I0510927

How People Change Organizations

How People Change Organizations

Transforming Systems through Presence,
Practice, and Projects

Kathy Cowan Sahadath

BUSINESS EXPERT PRESS

Leader in applied, concise business books

How People Change Organizations:
Transforming Systems through Presence, Practice, and Projects

Copyright © Business Expert Press, LLC, 2026.

Cover design by Cassandra Kronstedt

Interior design by S4Carlisle Publishing Services, Chennai, India

All rights reserved. No part of this publication may be reproduced, stored in a retrieval system, or transmitted in any form or by any means—electronic, mechanical, photocopy, recording, or any other except for brief quotations, not to exceed 400 words, without the prior permission of the publisher.

First published in 2026 by
Business Expert Press, LLC
222 East 46th Street, New York, NY 10017
www.businessexpertpress.com

ISBN-13: 978-1-60649-274-1 (paperback)
ISBN-13: 978-1-60649-433-2 (e-book)

Portfolio and Project Management Collection

First edition: 2026

10 9 8 7 6 5 4 3 2 1

EU SAFETY REPRESENTATIVE
Mare Nostrum Group B.V.
Doelen 72
4831 GR Breda
The Netherlands
gpsr@mare-nostrum.co.uk

Description

How People Change Organizations: Transforming Systems through Presence, Practice, and Projects is a timely guide for leaders navigating the human complexity of organizational change. In an era where transformation is often reduced to strategy decks, software rollouts, or restructuring plans, this book offers a deeper view: that real, lasting transformation begins with how leaders show up, in conversation, in reflection, and in relationship. Whether you're leading from the C-suite, a project team, or a change management office, you'll find tools, insights, and language to lead with greater empathy, alignment, and presence.

Grounded in systems thinking (Senge et al. 2015; Senge 1995), adult development theory, and real-world leadership practice, this book introduces a powerful integration model across project, change, and executive leadership roles. Through the ongoing narrative of the WynnTech case study, you'll explore how inclusive delivery, narrative sensemaking, and cultural modeling can transform not only outcomes but also the people and systems behind them. Ideal for project leaders, change agents, and executives alike, this book helps you lead transformation from the inside out, by centering people in everything you do.

Contents

List of Tables and Figures ix

Acknowledgments...xi

Introduction xiii

QuickStart Guide..xvii

PART 1   **Grounding Leadership in Presence and Reflection**....... **1**

Chapter 1   What It Really Means to Lead Transformation.................3

Chapter 2   Empathy as a Strategy—Leading Through Uncertainty...21

Chapter 3   Reflection as a Leadership Discipline 29

PART 2   **Building Trust and Culture Through Change** **41**

Chapter 4   Aligning Culture, Purpose, and Performance.................43

Chapter 5   Reframing Resistance and Rebuilding Trust...................53

Chapter 6   Making Sense Together: Storytelling, Listening, and
Dialogue..63

PART 3   **Leading from the Edge**... **75**

Chapter 7   Modeling the Change
You Seek...77

Chapter 8   Learning at the Edge: Vulnerability and Growth
in Leadership 85

PART 4   **Embedding Systemic Change**..................................... **93**

Chapter 9   Centering People in Digital Transformation 95

Chapter 10   The Inner Work of Systemic Change 101

Appendixes

Appendix A   *Leadership Integration Model in Practice* 111

Appendix B   *Dual-Lens Framework Overview*.....................................115

Appendix C   *The Reflection Compass*..119

Appendix D   *The WynnTech Case Study* 121

Appendix E   *Reflective Dialogue Guide* 127

Glossary 129
References 131
Back Cover Story 133
About the Author 135
Index 137

List of Tables and Figures

Tables

Table 1.1   The power of integrated leadership 7

Table 1.2   Myths of transformation 13

Table 2.1   Leadership integration spotlight 24

Table 2.2   Empathy action bridge 24

Table 3.1   The reflection compass 32

Table 3.2   Leadership integration spotlight—reflection in action 36

Table 3.3   Tool selection guide 38

Table 4.1   The alignment arc in practice 49

Table 5.1   Trust diagnostic and conversation audit 59

Table 5.2   Reflection in action at WynnTech 59

Table 6.1   Reflective dialogue guide 68

Table 7.1   Leadership signals map 81

Table 8.1   Dual-lens conversation reflection prompts 88

Table 8.2   Aligning with the growth zone reflection matrix............89

Table 9.1   People-centered leadership 98

Table 10.1   Inner work driving systemic change 104

Figures

Figure 1.1   The Leadership Integration Model 5

Figure 1.2   Dual-Lens Framework for people-centered leadership 8

Figure 1.3   Integrated leadership: people-centered transformation.....12

Figure 1.4   The weave of transformation 12

Figure 1.5   Compass icon..16

Figure 1.6   The reflective compass tool...17

Acknowledgments

This book came to life through the encouragement, insight, and generosity of many people.

To my family, friends, colleagues, and collaborators, past and present, thank you for the rich conversations, thoughtful reflections, and shared commitment to purposeful leadership. Your perspectives and feedback shaped both the ideas and the tools that appear throughout these pages.

To the leaders and teams I've had the privilege to work with, your openness, courage, and curiosity in leading through change have been my greatest teachers. The stories and experiences you shared brought depth and authenticity to every chapter, grounding theory in lived practice.

To the editorial and publishing team, thank you for your guidance, care, and skill in helping bring this vision to the page. And to the readers, thank you for your time, trust, and willingness to engage in these ideas. May this book serve as a thoughtful companion in your own leadership practice, sparking new insights and meaningful change.

Finally, to my greatest supporters, my late husband Cyril, and my remarkable son Casey, thank you for your unwavering belief in me. Your love, wisdom, and curiosity continue to shape how I see the world.

Introduction

Change in organizations rarely begins with a grand announcement. It often starts quietly, with a conversation, a question, or a moment when someone decides to see things differently. In complex systems, presence matters as much as planning. This book begins with a simple premise: Transformation starts with people, not processes.

Leading through change today requires more than strategies, milestones, or implementation frameworks. It calls for leaders at every level to develop the capacity for awareness, empathy, and trust, qualities that help people find their way through uncertainty together. This book explores what it means to lead transformation from the inside out, through presence, practice, and relationship.

This book is for project managers, change practitioners, and executives who find themselves leading without a clear map. It offers a way of seeing leadership as conversation, where reflection, dialogue, and action work together to align purpose and performance.

Two foundational frameworks anchor this approach. The first, the **Leadership Integration Model**, connects the actions of project, change, and executive leaders to ensure alignment across the organization. The second, the **Dual-Lens Framework**, helps leaders attend to both their internal experience (Lens 1) and the external dynamics of systems, structures, and relationships (Lens 2). Together, these frameworks show how individual awareness and systemic action reinforce one another.

Throughout the book, you'll follow the **WynnTech** story, where three leaders, **Nia**, **Marcus**, and **Elena,** navigate real tensions between culture, strategy, and human experience. Their journey illustrates how theory becomes practice and how dialogue becomes transformation. You will see how reflection translates into action and how leadership presence shapes outcomes.

At the center of the WynnTech story are three leaders whose distinct perspectives illuminate the human side of transformation. **Nia Thompson**, a project manager known for her inclusive delivery approach, champions adaptive planning and psychological safety. **Marcus Lee**, the change leader, serves as the organization's storyteller and facilitator of dialogue, helping teams reconnect with shared purpose. **Elena Patel**, WynnTech's chief operating officer, embodies the executive journey from control to presence, learning to lead through curiosity and vulnerability rather than certainty. Together, their experiences reveal how alignment, empathy, and reflection translate complex systems into real organizational change.

WynnTech itself, a mid-sized technology firm undertaking a sweeping digital transformation, serves as the book's living case. What begins as a modernization project evolves into a cultural reawakening, where leaders learn that change is sustained not through process alone but also through the quality of their relationships and conversations. A fuller version of their story appears in Appendix D.

The frameworks, tools, and reflective practices in these pages are designed to help you experiment in your own context. You don't need to master everything at once. The aim is not perfection but practice, small, steady steps that strengthen your ability to lead through complexity.

Navigating the Tools

You'll encounter a range of frameworks and visuals as you move through the chapters. Each one is an entry point for reflection rather than a checklist to complete. The goal is to help you slow down, notice patterns, and hold both the human and systemic dimensions of change.

If you begin to feel overwhelmed, return to the idea that leadership is relational. Every model and exercise is an invitation to a conversation, with yourself, your team, and the system around you.

Your Invitation

Transformation is not a linear process. It unfolds through the presence you bring to each moment and the courage to stay in dialogue when things are uncertain. You will find space here to reflect, reframe, and reconnect with your purpose as a leader of change.

As you turn the page, the next section, the **QuickStart Guide,** offers a simple orientation to help you begin. It provides a short overview of the core frameworks, the WynnTech storyline, and the learning tools that bring this book to life. Think of it as your map for the journey ahead. You don't need to remember every model or term; this guide is simply here to help you move through the book with confidence and clarity, one conversation at a time.

QuickStart Guide

Why This Guide

Change can feel complex, and leadership frameworks can sometimes add to that complexity instead of easing it. The purpose of this QuickStart Guide is to make the journey simpler. It highlights what you'll encounter in the chapters ahead, the frameworks, the storyline, and the reflective tools, so you can move at your own pace without feeling overwhelmed. Think of it as an orientation before we dive in, a way to begin with focus and ease.

1. Continuity with Book 1

This book builds on *Empowering Strategic Change*, expanding the Dual-Lens Framework and Leadership Integration Model into a deeper exploration of presence, practice, and projects. If you're joining the series here, you'll still find everything you need; this volume stands on its own while extending the ideas introduced earlier.

2. Core Frameworks

The two core frameworks, the **Leadership Integration Model** and the **Dual-Lens Framework,** work together to connect self-awareness with systemic change. The first aligns roles across project, change, and executive levels to ensure that culture, purpose, and performance move in the same direction. The second helps leaders balance internal reflection and external engagement. A detailed overview of the **Leadership Integration Model** appears in Appendix A. A detailed overview of the **Dual-Lens Framework**, including the five categories of inner experience and their conversational functions, appears in Appendix B for readers who want to explore the model in depth. These frameworks reappear throughout the chapters as mirrors for your own leadership practice. You'll see how each helps translate insight into coordinated action.

3. The Storyline

The **WynnTech** narrative provides a realistic thread through the book. You'll follow Nia, Marcus, and Elena as they face moments of alignment, resistance, and renewal in leading transformation. Their experiences mirror challenges many of us face, balancing strategy with empathy, systems with relationships, and urgency with reflection.

Each chapter uses their story to illustrate how people-centered transformation looks in practice. You can engage with it as a living case, using their insights to spark your own reflection.

4. The Learning Tools

Every chapter includes reflective elements designed to help you integrate what you're learning:

- **Host This Conversation** prompts invite dialogue around key ideas.
- **Spotlight Tables** and **Framework Figures** show how different leadership roles interact.

These are not assessments or performance measures; they are invitations to notice patterns, test insights, and strengthen the link between reflection and real-world leadership.

5. How to Navigate This Book

You can move through the chapters sequentially, or you can begin where your current challenge lies. Each chapter is designed to stand alone while building toward a cumulative understanding of how people change organizations.

At the end of Part 1, you'll find the **Tool Selection Guide**, a quick resource to help you decide where to focus if you're feeling uncertain about where to begin. Remember, you don't have to do everything—start where your leadership work feels most alive.

6. Tip for Readers

This book isn't meant to be a linear workbook. Think of it instead as a set of conversations. Take what serves you, leave what doesn't, and revisit the ideas that speak to your current leadership challenges. Reflection is most powerful when it meets you where you are.

7. Your Next Step

Begin where curiosity meets need. The next chapter explores how people, not processes, drive transformation that lasts. The frameworks ahead are not rules but invitations, to see more clearly, act more consciously, and lead change in ways that honor both people and purpose.

PART 1

Grounding Leadership in Presence and Reflection

Framework Preview

Part 1 lays the foundation for the two frameworks introduced at the start of the book. The *Leadership Integration Model* defines how project, change, and executive leaders connect across the system, while the *Dual-Lens Framework* helps us see the relationship between inner awareness and outward alignment. At *WynnTech*, these frameworks begin to surface as Nia, Marcus, and Elena confront early signs of disconnection and start to look beneath the surface of change.

As will be introduced in the *Weave of Transformation* (Figure 1.4), these two strands—structure and awareness—now move together through each chapter, revealing how reflection shapes coordination and how alignment deepens presence. Together, they shift our focus from managing change to cultivating shared purpose.

CHAPTER 1

What It Really Means to Lead Transformation

Transformation often falters not because strategies are flawed, but because leadership is fragmented. This chapter introduces the **Leadership Integration Model** and sets the stage for understanding how project, change, and executive leaders can align their efforts to create sustainable, people-centered transformation. It also prepares the ground for the **Dual-Lens Framework**, which shows how presence and conversation sustain the alignment that structure alone can't.

Learning Outcomes:

By the end of this chapter, you will be able to:

- Explain why transformation requires more than technical plans.
- Describe the roles of Project, Change, and Executive Leaders.
- Understand how the Leadership Integration Model reframes leadership as a collective practice.
- Apply reflective questions to your own leadership orientation.

Leadership Lens: The WynnTech Call to Align

Nia stared at the agenda, knowing the conversation ahead wasn't just about deadlines but about trust. Across the table, Elena's silence spoke volumes as Marcus weighed how to surface the tension no one wanted to name.

She could feel the tension the moment she stepped into the room.

A dozen faces sat waiting, some masked with polite anticipation, and others narrowed with frustration. At the far end, a senior executive stared at her over folded arms. The launch hadn't gone well. Reports

---

were delayed. A key stakeholder had walked. No one was saying it aloud, but the question was clear: Who was responsible?

Elena didn't speak right away. She closed her laptop, moved the agenda aside, and looked around the table. "Before we get into updates," she began, "Can we talk about how we're actually doing right now?"

It wasn't a strategy or a tactic. It was a choice to pause. To be present. To allow for truth. A long silence followed, then Marcus spoke. "I think we're all trying to keep the wheels moving, but there's a lot we haven't said."

This was the moment it shifted, not because someone had a better answer but because someone asked a better question.

Why Transformation Often Falters

Too often, transformation is treated as a technical exercise. We define the plan, assign responsibilities, launch the initiative, and move forward. But in real life, transformation doesn't move forward in straight lines. It moves in fits and starts, through emotional waves and fragile trust. It is shaped by relationships, not just milestones.

Transformation doesn't stall because leaders don't care. It stalls because they lead in silos. Project leads chase deliverables. Executives hold strategy. Change specialists manage engagement. Yet, without coordination, even strong efforts cancel each other out.

This chapter reframes transformation not as a single leader's burden but, instead, as a choreography of leadership, a collective practice that depends on integration.

The Leadership Integration Model

Introducing the Leadership Integration Model (Figure 1.1) is a way to see transformation as a shared ecosystem of three complementary roles:

- Project Leadership: Focused on delivery and adaptability
- Change Leadership: Focused on meaning-making and engagement
- Executive Leadership: Focused on culture, trust, and modeling

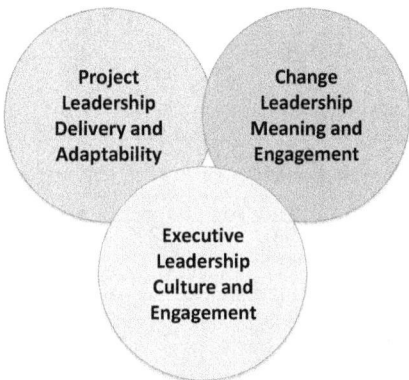

Figure 1.1 The Leadership Integration Model

Each role contributes something essential, but only together do they create sustainable transformation:

Nia: Project Leadership

As a project leader, Nia is responsible for making things happen. But she's not just chasing deliverables. She anchors timelines in inclusion, prioritizes psychological safety, and responds to tension with curiosity, not control.

Her questions sound like:

- Are we designing this process with people or to people?
- Are we adapting as we learn?
- Are we listening to resistance as data?

Nia represents leadership that integrates governance with empathy. A project isn't just a plan; it's a lived experience for those involved.

Marcus: Change Leadership

Marcus operates at the level of engagement, story, and meaning. He facilitates emotionally charged conversations, surfaces fears and aspirations, and invites people into shared authorship of change. His work is less visible, but no less critical.

Change doesn't land because it's explained. It lands because it's felt. His questions sound like:

- Are we naming what's really going on?
- Are we giving people language for the change?
- Are we creating safe space for disagreement?

Change leadership is often dismissed as soft, but, in reality, it is some of the hardest work to do well.

Elena: Executive Leadership

Elena holds the broader system. She knows culture is not shaped by slogans but, instead, by presence and consistency. She doesn't just communicate strategy, she embodies it.

Her questions sound like:

- How am I showing up?
- What does this moment need from me?
- Am I creating conditions for others to grow?

Executive leadership is less about control and more about credibility. And credibility is earned through humility, integrity, and courage.

For a detailed overview of the Leadership Integration Model, including its origins, role definitions, and application tools, see **Appendix A: Leadership Integration Model in Practice.** This chapter and the chapters ahead will explore how each leadership role engages with transformation differently, and together.

Leadership as Integration, Not Isolation

When leadership roles are siloed, organizations experience the ripple effects: Project plans move forward without emotional alignment, communication strategies lack delivery coordination, and executive signals are out of sync with lived culture. But when leadership is integrated, a different reality takes shape. Each role contributes to a shared culture of alignment and trust. Project leaders adapt their delivery to reflect equity and inclusion. Change leaders create space for meaning-making. Executives model the behaviors they want to see in others. Table 1.1 below illustrates the distinct contributions of each leadership role.

While this model explains who leads transformation, the Dual-Lens Framework explores how each leader shows up to that work

The Leadership Integration Model matters because transformation doesn't fail from lack of effort; it fails from fragmentation. Project leads deliver, but without cultural alignment. Change leads engage, but without operational support. Executives set vision, but without relational depth.

Only when these roles are practiced in concert, with shared values and reflective practice, does transformation become sustainable.

With the Integration Model defining the system of roles, the next framework turns to the inner and relational work that makes those roles effective.

The Dual-Lens Framework for People-Centered Leadership

To bring the Integration Model to life, leaders need a way to balance inner awareness with external action—that's the purpose of the **Dual-Lens Framework**. To lead people through uncertainty, tension, and systemic change, we need more than project plans or executive directives. We need leaders who are both internally grounded and externally attuned. The **Dual-Lens Framework** for people-centered leadership is a practical way to integrate inner presence with outer impact.

Table 1.1 The power of integrated leadership

Element	Project leader	Change leader	Executive leader
Purpose	Align delivery with people-first values	Translate purpose into shared meaning	Model values through consistent presence
Practice	Adaptive planning, inclusive governance	Storytelling, dialogue facilitation	Learning sessions, reflection modeling
Impact	Smoother execution, reduced resistance	Greater engagement, clearer narrative	Cultural shifts, enhanced trust

- **Lens 1: Internal Experience** focuses on the leader's inner world: emotional posture, mindset, presence, and awareness. It asks: Who am I being in this moment? It's the capacity to pause before reacting, to notice our assumptions, and to lead from clarity rather than fear.
- **Lens 2: External Conversation** focuses on the leader's role in shaping relationships and meaning. It asks: How am I creating alignment, trust, and understanding through what I say and how I listen? This is the realm of dialogue, sensemaking, and cultural coherence.

These two lenses (see Figure 1.2 below) are inseparable—each sharpens the other. A leader may be deeply self-aware but ineffective in dialogue or may be skilled in communication but unaware of their inner triggers. Transformation demands both.

When used together, the Dual-Lens Framework equips leaders to navigate complexity with intention. It moves us beyond reactive leadership toward reflective presence. It turns performance conversations into learning opportunities. It transforms meetings into meaning-making spaces.

While the Leadership Integration Model shows who contributes to transformation, the Dual-Lens Framework explains how leaders engage

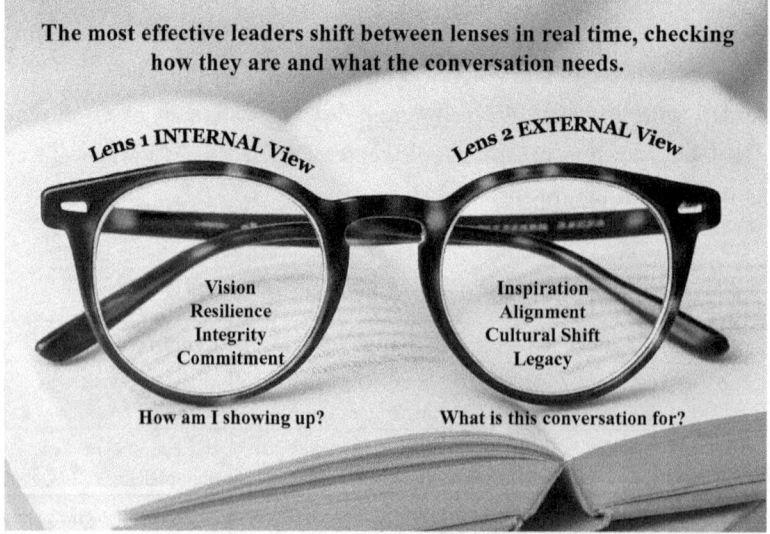

Figure 1.2 Dual-Lens Framework for people-centered leadership

in presence and conversation. Together, they form a cohesive foundation for people-centered change.

Choreographing Leadership: The Leadership Integration Model

Most organizations assign responsibility for transformation to individual leaders. A project sponsor. A change agent. A visionary executive. And yet, despite good intentions, the work often stalls, not because people don't care but because they're not working together. Project leads focus on deadlines. Executives focus on strategy. Change specialists try to hold the middle. But without coordination, even strong efforts can cancel each other out.

That's why this book introduces the **Leadership Integration Model,** a simple but powerful way to think about leadership as a systemic function. This model reframes transformation as a choreography of three complementary roles:

- **Project Leadership**: Focused on **delivery and adaptability**
- **Change Leadership**: Focused on **meaning-making and engagement**
- **Executive Leadership**: Focused on **culture, trust, and modeling**

Each role contributes something essential to the ecosystem of transformation. And each is explored through the lived experiences of our three narrative characters: Nia, Marcus, and Elena, who model these roles in action.

Let's take a closer look at how each role works together.

Nia: Project Leadership

As a project leader, Nia is responsible for making things happen. But she's not just chasing deliverables. She anchors timelines in inclusion, prioritizes psychological safety, and responds to tension with curiosity, not control. Her leadership asks:

- Are we designing this process with people or to people?

- Are we adapting as we learn?
- Are we listening to resistance as data?

Nia represents a form of leadership that integrates governance with empathy. She understands that a project isn't just a plan; it's a lived experience for those involved.

Marcus: Change Leadership

Marcus operates at the level of engagement, story, and meaning. He facilitates emotionally charged conversations, surfaces fears and aspirations, and invites people into shared authorship of change. His work is less visible, but no less critical.

Change doesn't land because it's explained; it lands because it's felt.

Through Marcus, we see how leadership becomes a sensemaking practice, one that honors uncertainty while building alignment.

- Are we naming what's really going on?
- Are we giving people language for the change?
- Are we creating safe space for disagreement?

Change leadership is often dismissed as soft, but in reality, it's one of the hardest things to do well.

Elena: Executive Leadership

Elena holds the broader system. She knows that culture is not shaped by slogans, but by presence, modeling, and consistency. She doesn't just communicate the strategy, she embodies it. She listens with openness, admits mistakes, and cultivates trust by being real.

Her questions sound like:

- How am I showing up?
- What does this moment need from me?
- Am I creating conditions for others to grow?

Elena teaches us that executive leadership is less about control and more about credibility. And credibility is earned through humility, integrity, and courage.

Integrating Presence and Impact: Where the Models Meet

The **Dual-Lens Framework** and the **Leadership Integration Model** are not separate ideas; they reinforce each other. The Dual-Lens approach gives each leader a way to pause and reflect:

- **Internally**: What am I bringing to this moment?
- **Externally**: How am I using my role to build trust, sense, and coherence?

Together, the two frameworks enable leaders at every level to transform not just systems but also relationships, conversations, and themselves. When used together, these lenses help leaders show up more intentionally and lead change more coherently, because transformation doesn't just require better planning; it also requires better presence.

Figure 1.3 illustrates how the Leadership Integration Model and the Dual-Lens Framework combine into an integrated practice of people-centered leadership—the system and the self-working as one. Appendix B expands on the Dual-Lens Framework introduced here, providing examples of how reflection and conversation intersect in practice.

The Weave of Transformation: Integrating Roles and Awareness

The connection between the *Leadership Integration Model* and the *Dual-Lens Framework* can be imagined as two strands woven through the entire book. Each chapter strengthens one strand while keeping it interdependent with the other, structure and awareness, system and self, action and reflection. This dynamic interplay is illustrated in Figure 1.4, which maps how the frameworks evolve and intersect across the leadership journey.

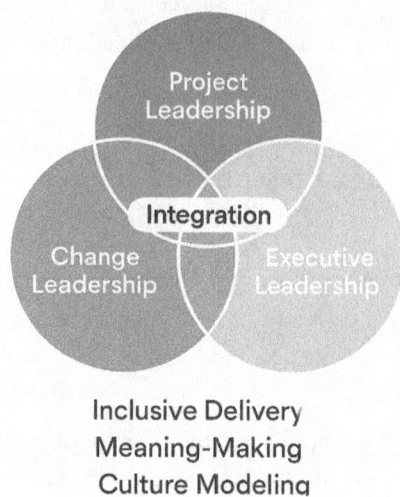

Inclusive Delivery
Meaning-Making
Culture Modeling

Figure 1.3 Integrated leadership: people-centered transformation

Leadership Integration Model (LIM)

Coordination. Accountability. Alignment . Shared Purpose

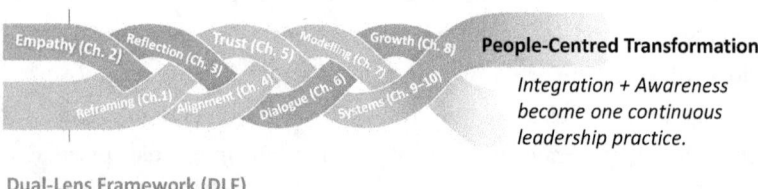

People-Centred Transformation

*Integration + Awareness
become one continuous
leadership practice.*

Dual-Lens Framework (DLF)

Presence. Reflection. Dialogue. Connection.

Figure 1.4 The weave of transformation

The *Leadership Integration Model* and *Dual-Lens Framework* operate as two interwoven strands of leadership practice. The weave begins in Chapter 1, where structure and awareness first meet; renews through learning in Chapter 8; and culminates in Part 4, where alignment and presence merge into a single practice of people-centered transformation.

Transformation Is Not a Project—It Is a Paradigm Shift

In many organizations, transformation is reduced to a program plan or a system overhaul. But true transformation demands a deeper kind of change, one that invites individuals, teams, and organizations to evolve not only how they work but also how they think, feel, and lead.

Transformation is not about replacing legacy systems. It's about renewing trust.

It's not about launching a new digital platform. It's about creating shared meaning.

And it's not about managing people through change; it's about inviting them into it. True transformation changes how people experience work. It shifts mindsets (see Table 1.2), not just workflows. And it invites everyone into the ongoing process of cultural evolution, not as spectators but as participants.

This book challenges three common assumptions about transformation:

- **From Systems-First to People-First:** Most plans start with technology, structure, or strategy. But culture eats all three for breakfast. People's emotional and psychological readiness is the real determinant of change.
- **From Deliverables to Dialogue:** Deadlines and Key Performance Indicators (KPIs) matter. But they don't replace the need for conversation. Transformation lives and dies in the quality of connection between people.
- **From Control to Co-creation:** Top-down mandates may create short-term compliance. But long-term change requires ownership, and ownership grows through co-creation.

Table 1.2 Myths of transformation

Myth	Reality
Change is a technical rollout.	Change is a cultural shift.
Resistance is a problem to fix.	Resistance is a signal to explore.
Strategy drives transformation.	Relationships and trust sustain it.
Leaders need to have all the answers.	Leaders need to create space for dialogue.
People will follow if the plan is strong enough.	People engage when the purpose is shared and personal.

Unlearning these myths is essential for leaders who want to create lasting, people-centered change. This shift requires leaders to challenge three dominant assumptions that often derail meaningful change:

- From systems-first to people-first: Systems matter, but they are only as effective as the trust and engagement of those who use them.
- From deliverables to dialogue: Milestones track progress, but only dialogue creates understanding, buy-in, and shared purpose.
- From control to co-creation: Leaders who loosen control empower others to take ownership and innovate from within.

Transformation today is too often reduced to a strategy slide or a new platform rollout. But real transformation begins when leaders ask, What are we transforming into, and who must we become to get there together? Transformation is not about checking boxes; it's about changing culture. And culture is changed through conversation, empathy, and example.

Why the Human Element Gets Overlooked

Despite decades of literature on emotional intelligence, inclusion, and organizational culture, people still often become an afterthought in transformation plans. Why?

Because they're hard to quantify. Their reactions are unpredictable. Their experiences don't fit neatly into Gantt charts.

Three common tendencies contribute to this oversight:

- Human complexity is seen as a distraction: When under pressure to deliver, leaders often minimize the emotional and relational aspects of change.
- Emotional reactions are interpreted as resistance: In truth, they're often signals of unmet needs, unspoken fears, or unacknowledged wisdom.
- Leadership development is siloed from operational delivery: Project managers, change professionals, and executives are often trained in different frameworks and rarely speak a common language of leadership.

Yet it is precisely these human factors—trust, belonging, safety, and clarity—that determine whether transformation will flourish or falter.

When people feel seen, heard, and valued, they invest. When they feel invisible, they retreat.

Reflective Leadership Begins with You

I invite readers to reflect on which leadership roles you lean into and where your growth edge may lie. Use this scan to reflect on your natural leadership orientation and uncover areas for growth.

"When I think about my role in transformation, I tend to focus on…"
- ○ Delivery and execution
- ○ Story and engagement
- ○ Culture and modeling

When I feel discomfort, I tend to…
- ○ Press forward with the plan
- ○ Try to explain or reframe
- ○ Retreat or take control

These insights will help shape your journey through the book and through the transformation they are leading. What patterns do you notice in your own leadership? What happens when you feel uncertainty, urgency, or pushback? What do you believe about people?

Use these reflections to track your leadership growth throughout the book. You'll meet each of these roles again, in future chapters, with deeper tools to help you lead from the inside out.

Transformation Begins Here: The Reflective Compass Tool

Change doesn't begin with a plan; it begins with a pause. That's why this chapter invites you to explore the **Reflection Compass**: a simple yet powerful tool to strengthen your awareness and leadership alignment (Figure 1.5).

Figure 1.5 Compass icon

The compass includes four quadrants:

- **North—What Am I Noticing?**
  Tune into what's happening within you and around you. This could include energy shifts, tensions, signals of resistance, or moments of clarity.
- **South—What Am I Feeling?**
  Acknowledge the emotional undercurrent of a situation. Is there frustration, excitement, fear, or hope? Leadership presence begins with emotional fluency.
- **East—What Am I Assuming?**
  Surface the implicit beliefs or narratives you may be carrying. What story are you telling yourself, and is it helpful?
- **West—What Matters Most?**
  Reconnect with your values and purpose. What's at stake here? What do you want to stand for in this moment?

We will return to this in greater depth in Chapter 3 where reflection is explored as a leadership discipline. Use the compass (outlined in Figure 1.6 below) during team meetings, decision points, or personal reflection. Over time, it helps leaders integrate insight with action, turning pause into presence.

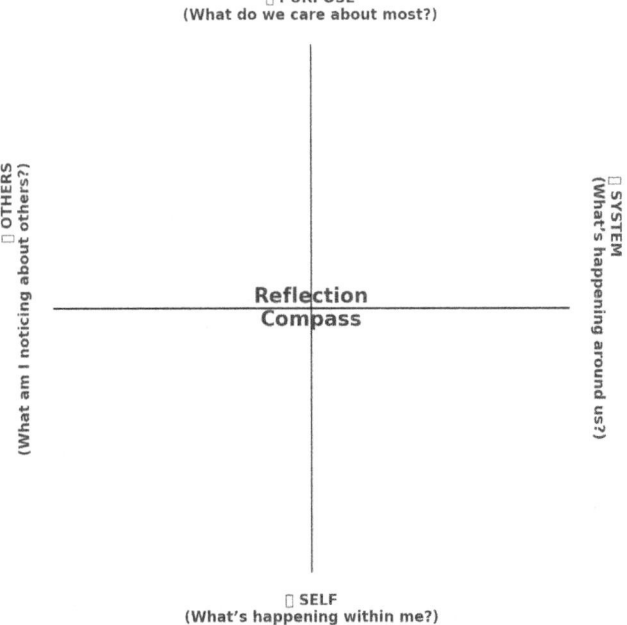

Figure 1.6 The reflective compass tool

Leadership Role Spotlight: Project, Change, and Executive Leadership

Each chapter in this book lifts up the distinct roles that shape people-centered transformation. In Chapter 1, the emphasis is on how these roles must interlock, not compete.

- **Project Leaders** (like Nia) create inclusive timelines and feedback structures that embody the values they aspire to deliver.
- **Change Leaders** (like Marcus) help people navigate the emotional and meaning-making aspects of transformation.
- **Executive Leaders** (like Elena) shape culture through consistent presence, not just policy.

When all three roles practice reflective integration, transformation becomes more than a plan. it becomes a practice.

Reflective Leadership Begins with You

Leadership integration doesn't start at the organizational level; it starts with individual awareness. Each leader must understand their own habits, instincts, and blind spots. This begins with asking powerful, reflective questions about how you show up in change. Are you drawn to execution over engagement? Do you withdraw when tensions rise? Are you modeling the behavior you want others to follow?

Self-inquiry like this isn't a detour from leadership—it is leadership. And it sets the stage for meaningful, people-centered transformation.

This chapter closes with an invitation, not to action but to reflection:

- What patterns do you notice in your own leadership when facing uncertainty?
- Which of the three leadership orientations do you naturally embody and which do you avoid?
- What conversations are waiting to happen in your organization but haven't yet found a host?

Host This Conversation—What It Really Means to Lead Transformation

Use these questions in a team dialogue, leadership roundtable, or coaching session to explore the themes from Chapter 1. Support shared understanding of people-centered transformation and each leader's role within it.

Conversation Starters:

- **In what ways have we experienced transformation efforts that were "systems-first" rather than "people-first"? How did it impact us?**
- **Which leadership roles, project, change, or executive tend to dominate in our organization's change efforts? Which are underrepresented?**
- **Where are we currently working in alignment and where are our leadership efforts fragmented?**

- **What conversations are we avoiding that could bring more coherence to our change efforts?**

Chapter Close: Why This Book Matters Now

Transformation has never been more necessary or more misunderstood. In an age of complexity, polarization, and burnout, it's tempting to respond with more strategy, more structure, and more urgency. But transformation won't happen faster by pushing harder. It will happen by leading deeper.

This book is your invitation to do just that. To lead with empathy. To listen before solving. To reflect before reacting. And to remember that what we change must work for people. Leading transformation requires more than well-aligned roles and reflective tools; it requires the emotional courage to meet people where they are. As we've seen, transformation is human work. And at the center of that work is empathy. Empathy is not a soft skill; it is a strategic capacity. It helps us decode resistance, build psychological safety, and navigate complexity with compassion rather than control. In the next chapter, we'll explore how empathy becomes a leadership strategy for uncertain times, one that turns listening into leverage and presence into power.

Looking Ahead: Weaving Presence and Practice

The chapters that follow build directly on the two frameworks introduced here. The **Leadership Integration Model** shows *who* leads transformation by aligning project, change, and executive leadership roles around shared purpose. The **Dual-Lens Framework** shows *how* leaders engage through awareness and dialogue, balancing internal reflection with external connection.

Together, they create a living system of leadership. Structural alignment becomes sustainable only when grounded in personal presence; individual reflection gains power when anchored in shared action. Across the pages ahead, these two frameworks will appear intertwined.

By the time we reach the final chapters, the two frameworks will merge fully into a single practice of **people-centered transformation,** leadership that integrates who we are with how we lead.

CHAPTER 2

Empathy as a Strategy— Leading Through Uncertainty

Empathy is not just a personal trait; it is a strategic capacity that enables leaders to navigate uncertainty, unlock resistance, and build trust. This chapter explores how project, change, and executive leaders apply empathy differently and how the Empathy Action Bridge and Dual-Lens Framework can help turn emotional awareness into adaptive action.

Learning Outcomes:

By the end of this chapter, you will be able to:

- Recognize empathy as a strategic leadership function, not just a soft skill.
- Explain how empathy plays out across the three roles in the Leadership Integration Model.
- Apply the Empathy Action Bridge to move from listening to adaptive response.
- Use the Dual-Lens Framework to reflect on empathy in both internal stance and external conversation.

Leadership Lens: Marcus and the Monday Stand-Up

What began as a simple system upgrade revealed tangled dependencies no one had anticipated. Every decision seemed to unravel three more, and the leaders realized they weren't just changing technology; they were changing how WynnTech worked.

The room was quiet, even for a Monday. Marcus looked around the circle of team leads, sensing the hesitation hanging in the air. A new system update was going live that week, and although timelines were technically on track, the energy was off. Some spoke in clipped tones; others avoided eye contact altogether.

"I know there's a lot in motion," Marcus said gently. "But I'd like to check in, not on the plan, but on how we're doing in the middle of it."

He paused. One manager, visibly tense, spoke up: "Honestly? We're tired. People are confused. Some are worried they'll be left behind."

That moment changed the course of the meeting. They didn't finish the agenda. Instead, they talked. They clarified expectations, surfaced anxieties, and agreed to adjust a few rollout milestones. And for the first time in weeks, Marcus felt the shift, not in process, but in trust.

While each leadership role expresses empathy differently, the shared intent is clear: to center people and cultivate trust in times of change. This approach aligns with growing research on transformational and inclusive leadership, where empathy is seen not only as an interpersonal strength but also as a cultural and systemic lever.

Recent studies highlight how empathy, emotional expression, and values-based leadership foster trust, belonging, and engagement in complex organizational settings. Inclusive leadership, defined by openness, accessibility, and commitment to fairness, has been shown to directly impact team psychological safety and performance (Randel et al. 2018). Similarly, transformational leaders who practice individualized consideration and shared vision tend to unlock higher creativity and resilience within teams (Bass and Riggio 2006). These findings reinforce the foundation of the Leadership Integration Model and Dual-Lens Framework, where empathy bridges the inner stance of the leader with the outer experience of the system.

Empathy as a Strategic Capacity

Empathy is often described as a personal strength or moral quality. But in the context of transformation, empathy is a strategic leadership skill, one that helps leaders navigate uncertainty, unlock resistance, and build cultures of safety and adaptability.

Rather than a soft gesture, empathy functions as an organizational muscle, reaching across silos, detecting unspoken barriers, and enabling adaptive action. When practiced intentionally, empathy supports resilience, accelerates trust, and creates the psychological space for change to take root.

This chapter explores empathy not as performance but as presence. It considers how each leadership role in the Leadership Integration Model—project, change, and executive—can engage empathy not just emotionally, but also operationally, to lead people through change with clarity, compassion, and courage. Empathy is not a one-size-fits-all behavior. Its expression, and its strategic impact, varies depending on your leadership role and context. That's where the Leadership Integration Model provides clarity. This model highlights three interconnected leadership roles essential to people-centered transformation:

- Project Leaders focus on delivery and adaptability.
- Change Leaders focus on meaning-making and emotional engagement.
- Executive Leaders focus on culture, trust, and modeling values.

Each of these roles engages with empathy differently because their vantage points and responsibilities are different. Yet all three are required to cultivate an environment where transformation is possible and sustainable.

The following table shows how empathy can become a practical tool for listening, aligning, and adjusting, whether you're facilitating a stand-up, reframing resistance, or listening across a system. These examples illustrate how the model comes to life, not just in theory but also in the day-to-day realities of leadership practice.

Leadership Integration Spotlight: Empathy in Action

Empathy plays out differently across leadership roles, but, in every case, it becomes a lever for insight, alignment, and forward movement (Table 2.1).

Table 2.1 Leadership integration spotlight

Leadership role	Empathy in action
Project Leader (Nia)	Adjusts daily stand-ups to include emotional check-ins. Balances pressure for delivery with creating space for uncertainty and vulnerability.
Change Leader (Marcus)	Facilitates open forums and uses story and metaphor to make the emotional reality of change visible. Reframes resistance as a signal of care.
Executive Leader (Elena)	Hosts listening sessions. Shares her own uncertainty to model psychological safety. Uses empathy to understand system-wide patterns beneath surface resistance.

Table 2.2 Empathy action bridge

Step	Strategic capacity	Description
1. Empathic Listening	Attune	Attend to what is being said, and what's not being said. Listen for tone, tension, and silence.
2. Pattern Recognition	Sense	Notice repeated fears, unmet needs, or signs of disconnection. Look for common threads across teams, stories, or feedback.
3. Adaptive Action	Respond	Adjust plans, priorities, or communication strategies to meaningfully respond to what's emerging.

Empathy, when practiced with intention, becomes more than a feeling; it becomes a leadership function. But what bridges the gap between caring and doing? Between understanding and adapting? The answer lies in the leader's ability to turn emotional awareness into responsive action.

The Empathy Action Bridge

The Empathy Action Bridge offers a simple but powerful way to guide that transformation. This tool operationalizes empathy, showing how to move from emotional signals to strategic adaptation in three steps: listen, sense, respond. It emphasizes that empathy alone is not enough; it must lead to insight and, ultimately, to adaptive action. This framework illustrates (Table 2.2) how empathetic listening becomes a bridge between emotional reality and strategic response.

Empathy without strategy can feel aimless. Strategy without empathy can feel imposed. The bridge between the two is where transformation gains traction.

Case in Point: Elena's Listening Tour

Elena, our executive sponsor from WynnTech, began hearing hallway chatter about "low morale" and "change fatigue." Rather than relying solely on reports, she scheduled informal listening sessions with teams across the company.

During these sessions, she practiced empathic listening, simply inviting people to share how the changes were affecting them, what they were hopeful about and what they feared. She didn't defend the strategy; she listened.

Over the course of these sessions, Elena noticed a recurring pattern: Many employees felt that decisions were being made "above them" without transparency or context. A sense of powerlessness had taken root.

Elena brought this insight to the leadership team and proposed an adaptive action: hosting monthly town halls led by cross-functional voices, where project leads could explain not just the "what" but the "why" of major changes. She also introduced a "You Said, We Did" feedback loop to close the communication gap.

Within a few months, the tone had shifted. Engagement scores improved. Employees began to express not just frustration but also curiosity. And Elena's reputation as a trusted leader grew, not because she had all the answers but because she chose to listen with purpose.

Empathy without strategy can feel aimless. Strategy without empathy can feel imposed. The bridge between the two is where transformation gains traction.

Reflection Prompts Using the Dual-Lens Framework

Turning empathy into action begins with noticing—what we hear from others and what we feel within ourselves. The Empathy Action Bridge helps leaders move from emotional signals to meaningful responses. But sustaining this kind of leadership requires more than a one-time adjustment; it requires ongoing reflection.

That's where the Dual-Lens Framework comes in. This tool invites leaders to pause and consider both their internal experience (how they are showing up) and their external conversational function (how they are engaging with others). Reflection is not just a private act; it is a leadership discipline that shapes culture, trust, and alignment.

Use the prompts that follow to strengthen your ability to lead with empathy, intention, and strategic clarity.

> Lens 1—Internal Experience:
> - When I encounter uncertainty, do I default to control, detachment, or connection?
> - What emotions do I find most difficult to name or hold, for myself or others?
>
> Lens 2—External Function:
> - In my recent conversations, was I trying to inform, or to understand?
> - What space did I create for others to speak freely without defensiveness?

These questions help leaders check their inner stance while tuning into the relational function of their conversations.

Practice in Action: Reframe a Meeting

Choose one upcoming meeting and incorporate an intentional "empathy moment." Begin with a check-in prompt like:

- "What's one word that describes how you're showing up today?"
- "What's a recent challenge that surprised you?"

Observe how this changes the tone, energy, and quality of interaction and how it surfaces concerns that may otherwise remain hidden.

Host This Conversation

Consider this prompt for peer or team reflection:

- **"Where in our organization are we asking for compliance instead of listening for concerns?"**
- **"What emotional realities might be shaping our team's behavior right now, and are we making space for them?"**

Use this in team huddles, learning sessions, or retrospective meetings. Listen not just for what is said but also for what is surfacing underneath.

Chapter Close: From Empathy to Reflection

Empathy allows us to step into uncertainty with others, to feel what's unspoken, to adjust when the path forward is unclear, and to lead with trust rather than control. It's not just a trait but a strategic stance: one that helps leaders translate emotional insight into meaningful action.

Yet empathy alone is not enough. To sustain trust, navigate ambiguity, and grow as a people-centered leader, we must also look inward.

That's where reflection comes in.

Reflection isn't a pause in leadership—it is leadership. It's how we metabolize complexity, confront our biases, learn from resistance, and integrate our values with our actions. Whether you're responding to tension in a team or navigating your own uncertainty, disciplined reflection is what allows empathy to become insight, and insight to become transformation.

In the next chapter, we explore reflection as a leadership discipline, one that strengthens presence, deepens perspective, and supports you in leading from the inside out.

CHAPTER 3

Reflection as a Leadership Discipline

Reflection is not a pause from leadership—it is leadership. This chapter introduces reflection as a strategic discipline that strengthens presence, builds trust, and helps leaders make sense of complexity. The Reflection Compass provides a practical way to embed reflection into daily leadership practice, supported by the Dual-Lens Framework.

Learning Outcomes:

By the end of this chapter, you will be able to:

- Explain why reflection is essential in transformation and complexity.
- Use the Reflection Compass to integrate self-awareness with systemic awareness.
- Apply reflection across project, change, and executive leadership roles.
- Connect reflection to the Dual-Lens Framework for intentional sensemaking.

Leadership Lens: The Power of Pause

The new initiative was barely announced before the rumors started. Employees whispered about job cuts, while project teams felt the growing divide between leadership's vision and their daily reality.

Marcus scrolled through the stakeholder notes on his tablet, his fingers hovering over the screen. The meeting had ended hours ago, but his body still carried the tension.

Halfway through, one of the senior managers had raised a concern about timelines. "You keep saying we're on track," she'd said, voice steady but sharp, "but no one on my team feels ready for this rollout."

Marcus remembered his immediate reaction: a flash of defensiveness, the instinct to justify, to protect the plan. But then he'd caught himself. He'd noticed the rigidity in his shoulders, the rising speed of his breath. Instead of speaking, he'd paused and listened, really listened.

Later, as he replayed the conversation in his mind, Marcus realized that pause had been the turning point. Rather than escalating into conflict, the discussion had opened a new door: People began sharing what wasn't working. Gaps in training. Confusion about the new reporting structure. Underlying fears about job security.

For Marcus, this wasn't just about adjusting project plans. It was about holding space for meaning. His role wasn't to have all the answers; it was to ask better questions, to see beneath the surface.

This was reflective leadership in action. What Marcus experienced in that meeting is at the heart of reflective leadership, pausing long enough to see more, so you can lead more effectively. To make sense of change, leaders must slow down to notice not just what is happening around them but also what is happening within them.

The Reflection Compass Tool

In the pace of modern transformation, reflection often gets sidelined. Under pressure to deliver outcomes quickly, leaders are rewarded for action, decisiveness, and speed. Yet without pausing to notice what's emerging, in ourselves, our teams, and our systems, we risk missing critical signals that shape success or failure. The Reflection Compass was designed to slow the moment down, making reflection a practical discipline rather than a luxury.

In complex transformations, reflection isn't a solo exercise. It's a discipline embedded into collective practice. The Reflection Compass is designed to help people-centered leaders build reflective capacity by intentionally scanning four key domains of experience: Self, Others, System, and Purpose (you will find a complete copy of the Reflection Compass Tool in Appendix C). In the midst of complex change, leaders often default to familiar responses without noticing the assumptions, pressures, or blind spots driving their actions. This tool slows the moment down, allowing for grounded insight and renewed intentionality.

Moments like this show why reflection isn't optional in transformation and it also needs structure. The Reflection Compass offers one way to make this pause intentional.

How to Use the Reflection Compass

Use this compass during or after significant decisions, emotionally charged meetings, or project turning points. Ask yourself the guiding questions in each quadrant to explore your leadership stance and uncover new insight. You can write responses in a journal, share them in peer reflection, or use them to guide a coaching conversation.

The **Reflection Compass** operationalizes this by helping leaders pause, orient, and act intentionally, even in the middle of pressure. It guides you to ask:

- What's happening inside me?
- What's unfolding around me?
- What's emerging across the system?
- How does this connect to our shared purpose?

By practicing reflection across these dimensions, leaders build capacity to integrate presence with practice. The following sections introduce the tool and show how it connects to empathy, alignment, and systemic transformation.

Reflection isn't just a pause; it's an orientation tool. In complex transformations, leaders need ways to ground themselves when uncertainty

Table 3.1 The reflection compass

Compass point—anchor	Key question	Purpose
Self	What's happening inside me right now?	Cultivate presence and self-awareness
Others	What's unfolding between us?	Understand relational dynamics
System	What's shifting around us?	Notice wider patterns and dependencies
Purpose	What are we here to achieve?	Reconnect decisions to shared goals

feels overwhelming. The Reflection Compass (shown in Table 3.1) provides four simple anchors.

Here's an example with Elena at the WynnTech Board Update:

Elena, the executive sponsor for WynnTech's transformation program, was preparing for a tense board update. Stakeholders were nervous; rumors of budget cuts were circulating. Before stepping into the room, Elena paused and oriented using the **Reflection Compass**:

- **Self**: "I'm carrying anxiety about being challenged, but I also trust the team."
- **Others**: "Board members are protective of their divisions; their questions may mask fear."
- **System**: "Budget rumors are amplifying stress; this isn't just about project delivery."
- **Purpose**: "My role is to build confidence and clarity, not defend every detail."

Grounded by this reflection, Elena opened the session by naming the uncertainty everyone felt and inviting questions openly. Tension eased, and collaboration deepened. The Reflection Compass translates these moments of pause into a structured practice leaders can use to navigate uncertainty with clarity.

While the Reflection Compass offers a practical guide, research across leadership, inclusion, and learning underscores why reflection is essential in complex systems. We return to the Reflection Compass later in Part 4, connecting it to systemic transformation.

Core Concepts and Framing

At the heart of systems leadership is the ability to see patterns others miss. In complex environments, single events rarely tell the whole story. Reflective leaders learn to step back and connect dots across seemingly unrelated dynamics, noticing shifts in team morale, repeated feedback from stakeholders, or subtle changes in system behavior. By making these patterns visible, leaders unlock leverage points that drive alignment, foster innovation, and build trust across the organization.

Reflection in leadership is often misunderstood. It's dismissed as introspection, or worse, as hesitation, a luxury in fast-paced transformation environments. But research tells a different story.

Leaders operating in high-change, high-stakes systems succeed not because they know more but because they see more (Petrie 2014). They notice patterns, ask better questions, and create the conditions for others to surface insights that matter. Reflection becomes a discipline, a strategic capacity that allows leaders to:

- Make sense of complexity before acting within it.
- Bridge inner awareness and outer impact, what we call the alignment of "presence and practice."
- Create psychological safety by signaling curiosity over certainty (Edmondson 2019).
- Adapt more effectively by turning insights into shared learning loops (Argyris and Schön 1978).

Transformational leadership research reinforces this need for reflective capacity. Studies on inclusive leadership (Randel et al. 2018) demonstrate that when leaders pause to notice lived experiences and create meaning from them, they foster stronger engagement, innovation, and belonging.

Reflection, then, is not a pause from leadership. It *is* leadership.

Connecting to the Models

Remember, our Leadership Integration Model introduced in Chapter 1 highlights three essential roles in transformation:

- Project Leaders—Navigating delivery, adaptability, and resources
- Change Leaders—Translating meaning, engagement, and alignment
- Executive Leaders—Shaping trust, culture, and systemic coherence

Reflection operates differently across these roles, but it's nonnegotiable for all of them. Without reflective capacity, project leaders over-index on delivery at the expense of culture. Change leaders default to process instead of meaning. Executives drive alignment without trust.

While reflection shapes each leadership role differently, it becomes most powerful when viewed through two complementary lenses.

This is where the Dual-Lens Framework becomes practical:

- Lens 1—Internal Experience: How do I show up in this moment? What drives my stance? What am I missing?
- Lens 2—External Conversation: What's unfolding between us? Where is meaning being made or lost? What space am I creating for others?

By holding these two lenses together, leaders become more intentional sensemakers not just better decision-makers. Reflection turns reaction into response and response into alignment.

Reflection strengthens each leadership role differently but consistently creates a shared language of alignment. This integration comes to life in how leaders respond in real time. Consider Nia's experience during a high-stakes escalation call.

Case in Point: Nia's Insights

Nia, our senior project leader, sat in yet another escalation call about training gaps. Two departments were openly frustrated. Deadlines were slipping.

In previous projects, Nia might have tightened control: reassigning tasks, enforcing timelines, and signaling urgency. However, this time, she decided to try something different.

Before responding, she pulled out her notebook and ran through the **Reflection Compass**.

- **Self**: "I feel pressured to defend the plan, but what I want is trust."
- **Others**: "They're signaling fear and confusion, not resistance."
- **System**: "The rollout isn't failing, our communication is."
- **Purpose**: "If success depends on adoption, forcing speed undermines everything."

When Nia spoke, her tone had shifted:

"I hear the frustration. Can we step back and map the training gaps together? Let's find where we can create support without losing momentum."

The conversation transformed. What could have become a battle over deadlines became a collaborative problem-solving moment.

This is the work of reflection: slowing down to see more, so you can move forward together.

Leadership Integration Spotlight—Reflection in Action

Transformation doesn't happen in isolation; it lives in the everyday choices leaders make. The following snapshot (Table 3.2) highlights how project, change, and executive leaders bring empathy into action in their unique roles while contributing to a shared cultural shift. In the midst of Wynn-Tech's transformation, the weight of uncertainty shows up differently for each leader. For Nia, it surfaces in tense project stand-ups; for Marcus, in hushed conversations about resistance; and, for Elena, in the quiet anxieties behind performance metrics. The way each of them leans into empathy becomes a catalyst for alignment and trust across the organization.

Reflective discipline unlocks different insights at each leadership level:

- For **project leaders**, it surfaces delivery risks hidden in unspoken stress.

Table 3.2 Leadership integration spotlight—reflection in action

Leadership role	Reflection in action
Project Leader (Nia)	Builds "pause moments" into project stand-ups, inviting emotional check-ins alongside progress updates. Uses reflection to balance delivery pressures with team well-being.
Change Leader (Marcus)	Creates sensemaking sessions where employees explore "what this change means for me." Reflects openly on his own uncertainties to normalize adaptive learning.
Executive Leader (Elena)	Hosts quarterly "listening forums" with cross-functional teams to understand hidden system tensions. Uses reflective insights to guide governance decisions that align values with strategy.

- For **change leaders**, it deepens meaning and reframes resistance as care.
- For **executive leaders**, it connects decisions to culture and trust-building.

Building reflective capacity across these roles allows leaders to ground action in awareness. The Dual-Lens Framework supports this integration.

Host This Conversation

Use this prompt to engage your team or peers in a reflective dialogue that integrates presence, practice, and purpose:

- **"Where are we moving faster than our understanding?"**
- **"What assumptions about this transformation have we not surfaced yet?"**
- **"How might pausing together change what we choose to do next?"**

This conversation encourages collective reflection, creating space for psychological safety and deeper shared sensemaking before jumping to action.

Chapter Close: From Reflection to Alignment

Reflection is more than a personal practice; it becomes a collective discipline when shared across teams and systems. In transformation, leaders who cultivate reflective habits not only deepen their own awareness but also model a way of working that builds trust, coherence, and resilience.

Reflection surfaces hidden assumptions, challenges unspoken narratives, and creates the space where meaning can be co-created. In doing so, it transforms leadership from a reactive posture to an intentional choreography of presence and purpose.

This prepares us for the next challenge: aligning culture, purpose, and performance. If reflection shows us what matters and where we stand, alignment ensures we move together toward shared goals. In Chapter 4, we explore how leaders can connect personal insights with organizational realities, fostering cultures where values, strategy, and human experience converge.

Reflection is the practice that helps leaders make sense of complexity; Chapter 4 takes the next step, exploring how those insights shape culture, align purpose, and unlock performance at every level. Reflection opens our awareness; alignment turns awareness into coordinated action. In Chapter 4, we explore how leaders can connect these personal insights to organizational realities, fostering cultures where values, strategy, and human experience converge.

Tool Selection Guide

Choosing Where to Begin: A Quick Guide to Using the Tools

You've now met several tools and frameworks that invite reflection, connection, and clarity.

You don't need to use them all at once.

Start where your leadership journey needs the most attention, the tools will meet you there.

Each tool builds awareness from a different angle: self, relationships, systems, and action.

The guide below offers a few starting points depending on what you're noticing in your work right now (Table 3.3).

Table 3.3 Tool selection guide

If you're noticing...	Start with...	Why it helps
You're juggling many expectations and unsure where to focus.	**Leadership Integration Model (Chapter 1)**	Clarifies who leads what kind of change, project, change, and executive roles.
You're disconnected from your purpose or people feel distant.	**Empathy Action Bridge (Chapter 2)**	Rebuilds trust and connection by linking listening to shared understanding.
You're moving too fast to reflect or think clearly.	**Reflection Compass (Chapter 3)**	Brings you back to presence by pausing to notice Self, Others, System, and Purpose.
Your team feels misaligned or losing clarity of direction.	**Alignment Arc (Chapter 4)**	Connects what you say, measure, and do, turning purpose into performance.
Resistance or tension keeps surfacing in meetings.	**Trust Diagnostic (Chapter 5)**	Helps you see resistance as information and rebuild trust through small, visible actions.
Conversations are busy but not meaningful.	**Reflective Dialogue Guide (Chapter 6)**	Shifts talk from updates to insight, helping you listen to understand, not just respond.
You want to strengthen consistency and credibility.	**Leadership Signals Map (Chapter 7)**	Reveals how your daily actions signal values, or contradictions, to others.
You or your team is stretched thin and losing curiosity.	**Aligning with the Growth Zone Matrix (Chapter 8)**	Identifies where learning is happening, balancing support with stretch.
You're leading a digital or structural change.	**People-Centered Leadership (Chapter 9)**	Keeps the human experience visible during technology or process shifts.
You're ready to connect inner work to systemic change.	**Inner Work Inventory (Chapter 10)**	Integrates all frameworks—presence, practice, and projects—into one reflection.

How to Use This Guide

- **Start small.** Choose one tool that resonates with your current challenge.
- **Reflect in real time.** Use the prompts in that chapter to deepen learning as you lead.
- **Return and add.** As your awareness grows, new tools will become relevant.
- **Remember:** Transformation is cumulative. Each reflection builds the next one.

You don't need to master every framework; you only need to stay curious about what each reveals about how people change together.

PART 2

Building Trust and Culture Through Change

Framework Preview

In Part 2, the focus turns to how integration and awareness unfold through relationship. The ***Dual-Lens Framework*** comes forward here; listening, dialogue, and empathy become daily practices that sustain the structural alignment described by the ***Leadership Integration Model.*** Within ***WynnTech***, trust fractures and repairs through honest conversation; stories and shared meaning begin to reconnect people to purpose. Trust, story, and culture emerge as the connective tissue of transformation.

CHAPTER 4

Aligning Culture, Purpose, and Performance

Alignment links what we say we value, what we measure, and what we do. When culture, purpose, and performance drift apart, even capable teams lose coherence.

Learning Outcomes:

By the end of this chapter, you will be able to:

- Explain how alignment of culture, purpose, and performance sustains transformation.
- Apply the Leadership Integration Model to identify and correct misalignment.
- Use the Dual-Lens Framework to translate reflective awareness into coordinated action.

Leadership Lens: The Meeting That Shifted Everything

The most powerful transformations don't start with answers; they begin when someone dares to ask a better question.

By the second hour, the air in the WynnTech executive conference room was thick with frustration. Fluorescent lights hummed overhead, the stale scent of burnt coffee hung in the corner, and a dozen voices tangled in overlapping updates, rebuttals, and justifications.

Project deadlines had slipped again. Budgets were overrun. Teams were restless, and executives were growing impatient. But instead of clarity, the meeting had devolved into a slow unraveling, defensiveness masquerading as dialogue.

Nia sat at the far end of the table, jaw tight, fingers tapping against her notebook. The project timelines she'd meticulously planned were under siege from all sides. Every conversation seemed to come back to the same three demands: deliver faster, spend less, disrupt nothing. She'd been in enough of these sessions to know where they led, more pressure, less listening.

Beside her, Marcus leaned back in his chair, his expression unreadable but his eyes alert, scanning the room like he was listening for something beneath the words being spoken. He could hear it, the anxiety no one was naming. Years of working in change had taught him that frustration usually masked something deeper. But today, he couldn't quite find his opening.

At the head of the table, Elena clicked through slide after slide, her voice clipped, rehearsed, unwavering. As WynnTech's COO, she carried the weight of the board's expectations and the CEO's relentless push for transformation. And she hated these meetings, not the content, but the feeling of watching her leaders talk past each other.

By the 90-minute mark, the room was buzzing with heat, not energy. Nia tried again to flag the risks:

"If we push forward without rebuilding the backend architecture, we're going to break more than we fix."

Elena's jaw tightened.

"We don't have six months to refactor. The board expects visible progress in half that time."

Marcus leaned forward, sensing the moment slipping into another stalemate. He closed his laptop deliberately, the soft click cutting through the tension, and spoke into the rising noise.

"Can I ask us something different?"

The room stilled, not from agreement, but from surprise.

"What are we most afraid of losing if we get this wrong?"

Silence. The kind that lingers, stretches, makes everyone suddenly aware of their breath.

Nia's pen slipped from her fingers. Across the table, Elena stopped fiddling with her notes.

It was the question they'd all been circling but never naming. And slowly, one by one, they leaned into it.

"Trust," Nia said finally. "If this fails, my team stops believing me when I tell them to commit to another deadline."

Marcus nodded, his voice softer.

"Momentum. We've asked people to change so much already, if they stop seeing meaning in it, we lose them."

Elena stared down at her notes before closing the folder entirely.

"Credibility," she admitted quietly. "With the board. But also with each other. If we keep pushing for speed without alignment, we're the ones who look fragmented."

The shift was subtle but undeniable. Defenses lowered. Timelines paused. Someone cracked a window, and the sharp spring air drifted in.

From there, the conversation became something else. Marcus facilitated, gently pulling out threads, weaving them back into something coherent. Nia reframed risks as learning opportunities, mapping out what could actually flex without imploding the system. Elena began asking questions instead of giving directives, and the room gradually tilted from frustration toward collaboration.

This meeting marked the moment WynnTech realized its challenges were not technical gaps but cultural fractures, a misalignment between what leaders intended and what teams experienced. By the time they wrapped up, there was no magic solution. The deadlines were still ambitious. The architecture still fragile. But the leaders left aligned, not on the plan, but on the purpose. Outside the conference room, the hum of the office continued as if nothing had changed. But inside, something had shifted.

This was the moment WynnTech's transformation became less about implementing systems and more about rebuilding trust. Less about controlling the outcome and more about listening deeply enough to lead differently.

And none of them knew it yet, but this was also the conversation that would ripple through the organization for months to come, the first time the trio began practicing what it truly meant to lead change from the middle.

The challenges faced by Nia, Marcus, and Elena illustrate a common tension: When performance, culture, and purpose drift apart, even successful organizations risk losing coherence. This sets the stage for exploring what alignment really means in practice. What unfolded in that room captures the essence of alignment work: reconnecting performance pressures to shared purpose and lived values.

Core Concepts and Framing

Alignment is not consensus; it is coherence, the felt connection between strategy, culture, and daily behavior. Alignment isn't about everyone agreeing on everything. It's about ensuring that what we say we value, what we measure, and how we act are connected in ways people can believe in and rally around.

In Chapter 3, reflection helped leaders see misalignment; in Chapter 4, alignment becomes the act of restoring coherence. The Leadership Integration Model clarifies *who* within the system carries that responsibility, while the Dual-Lens Framework guides *how* leaders navigate the human tensions that surface when purpose, culture, and performance pull in different directions.

When organizations move through transformation without alignment:

- Strategies fail because people don't understand or believe in them.
- Culture statements feel hollow when behaviors contradict values.
- Performance metrics drive activity but disconnect from meaning.

Why Alignment Matters Now

In hybrid, fast-changing environments, leaders face constant trade-offs between efficiency and integrity. Alignment offers a way to hold both, grounding metrics in meaning. When people see clear through-lines between vision, values, and action, trust grows and performance follows.

In contrast, when alignment is intentionally cultivated:

- People experience coherence between purpose and performance.
- Teams make better decisions faster because trade-offs are explicit and shared.

- Leaders foster trust by inviting dialogue where misalignments can be safely named.

This is where the Leadership Integration Model and Dual-Lens Framework converge:

- Project Leaders translate purpose into delivery practices, ensuring the "why" drives the "what."
- Change Leaders act as sensemakers, facilitating conversations where conflicting perspectives can converge into shared meaning.
- Executive Leaders steward alignment between culture, strategy, and lived experience, modeling values from the top.

Through the Dual-Lens Framework:

- Lens 1—Internal Experience: Leaders pause to explore their own assumptions and motivations.
- Lens 2—External Conversation: Leaders facilitate dialogues that surface tensions and create shared understanding.

Alignment is not a one-time decision but an ongoing practice. It happens in leadership meetings, performance reviews, team check-ins, and hallway conversations. It's how organizations turn reflection into coordinated action.

To see these dynamics in action, consider WynnTech, an organization whose transformation journey demonstrates how quickly misalignments emerge when purpose, culture, and performance are out of sync.

Case in Progress: WynnTech's Tipping Point

WynnTech's transformation journey had been underway for months. New digital tools were rolling out, customer experience initiatives were in full swing, and cross-functional project teams had been set up to break old silos. Yet something wasn't landing.

During a leadership alignment session, Nia, WynnTech's senior project leader, voiced what many had been sensing:

"We're delivering a lot of activity," she said carefully, "but I'm not sure we've created shared meaning yet. Teams are asking why we're doing this, and I don't have a clear story to give them."

Marcus, the change leader, nodded. His stakeholder interviews had surfaced the same patterns. Different divisions understood transformation goals in wildly different ways: IT focused on efficiency, marketing cared about customer intimacy, and operations just wanted stability. Each perspective was valid, but, without a shared narrative, momentum was fragmenting.

Elena, the executive sponsor, sat quietly for a moment before speaking. "We can't afford to run parallel stories," she said. "If our culture and strategy don't align, we'll undermine our own progress."

That session became a catalyst. The leadership team introduced "alignment dialogues" facilitated conversations where project leads, change agents, and executives worked together to:

- Map purpose to delivery: Ensuring every project decision tied back to "why."
- Surface tensions openly: Treating disconnects as signals, not failures.
- Translate values into behaviors: Clarifying what customer-first, collaborative culture looked like day-to-day.

Over time, these rituals shifted the tone. Teams began to see themselves in the story rather than feeling like recipients of someone else's plan. Decisions moved faster because trade-offs were grounded in shared meaning.

The tipping point came when an unexpected system outage forced customer support to escalate. Instead of reverting to blame, cross-functional teams came together instinctively, guided by their renewed clarity on purpose and values. Performance recovered faster than expected, and trust deepened in the process.

WynnTech's experience demonstrates that alignment isn't an outcome—it's a practice. By continuously connecting purpose, culture, and performance, leaders transformed both their results and the lived experience of their people.

WynnTech's experience highlights a universal leadership challenge: translating personal insights and organizational realities into coordinated collective action. The Alignment Arc provides a simple, structured way to bridge these layers.

The Alignment Arc in Action

Transformation falters when personal insights remain disconnected from collective action. Leaders often sense the misalignment between stated values, evolving strategies, and lived organizational realities, but, without a way to integrate these dimensions, their reflections don't translate into meaningful change.

This is where the **Alignment Arc** comes in. It's a simple but powerful framing that connects three interdependent layers of transformation:

1. **Personal Insights**—What I notice in myself, my role, and my values.
2. **Organizational Realities**—What is unfolding around me across systems, structures, and relationships.
3. **Collective Action**—How we intentionally move together toward shared purpose and outcomes.

When leaders integrate these three layers (see Table 4.1), transformation stops being a set of abstract initiatives and becomes a lived practice.

Table 4.1 The alignment arc in practice

Alignment layer	Key focus	Guiding question	Risk if neglected
Personal values	Inner beliefs, ethics, leadership intent	What matters most to me right now?	Values disconnection; moral fatigue
Organizational purpose	Strategy, vision, culture, structures	How does this reflect who we are and where we're going?	Strategic drift; misalignment between talk and walk
Collective action	Implementation, coordination, ownership	How do we act together in a way that aligns with our shared goals?	Fragmentation; disengagement; performative change

Instead of reacting to misalignments, they actively surface them, name them, and reorient the system toward coherence.

This table provides a practical overview of the Alignment Arc and the tensions that emerge when any one layer is neglected. It is a useful anchor for the vignette that follows and a bridge to the tools and frameworks leaders can apply to create coherence in their organizations.

How the Models Intersect

The Leadership Integration Model and Dual-Lens Framework help operationalize the Alignment Arc:

- Leadership Integration Model
  Each role—Project Leader, Change Leader, and Executive Leader—anchors alignment differently.
  - Project Leaders translate insights into adaptive delivery decisions.
  - Change Leaders reframe uncertainty and meaning-making for teams.
  - Executive Leaders create cultural coherence and governance structures that reinforce shared purpose.
- Dual-Lens Framework
  The Alignment Arc also relies on leaders' ability to balance two lenses:
  - Lens 1—Internal Experience: Recognizing biases, fears, and opportunities within oneself
  - Lens 2—External Conversation: Building bridges through dialogue that connects personal meaning to organizational priorities

Together, these models show that alignment isn't achieved through top-down mandates. It's sustained through presence, reflective practice, and purposeful conversation at every level of leadership.

By using the Alignment Arc as a reflective tool, leaders create the conditions where trust, purpose, and performance can converge, unlocking organizational alignment that is both strategic and people-centered. With the Alignment Arc in mind, leaders can integrate reflection into everyday decisions using these guiding prompts.

Reflection Prompts Using the Dual-Lens Framework

These prompts help leaders integrate **Lens 1** (Internal Experience) and **Lens 2** (External Conversation) to foster alignment between personal insight and collective action:

Lens 1—Internal Experience

- How aligned am I with our shared purpose right now?
- What assumptions am I holding about others' intentions or constraints?
- Where am I reactive versus responsive in this situation?
- What personal values are being activated as I make this decision?

Lens 2—External Conversation

- What shared meaning is being built, or lost, in our current dialogue?
- Whose voices or experiences are shaping this narrative, and whose are missing?
- Where can I invite openness to surface unspoken concerns?
- How am I signaling curiosity rather than certainty to build trust?

Reflection deepens when shared. Use the following to host alignment conversations that build collective trust and meaning.

Host This Conversation

Bring your leadership, project, or transformation team together for a guided reflection. Follow up with these conversation starters:

- **Where are different teams or roles making different assumptions about what success looks like?**
- **How can we surface these assumptions safely, without judgment, so we can move forward together?**
- **What is one small shift we could make this month to better connect our shared purpose with day-to-day practice?**

Chapter Close: From Alignment to Adaptive Cultures

Alignment is not a static achievement; it is a continuous practice. It's the connective tissue between individual insight and collective action, where strategy and values are reconciled in real time. Through reflective practice, empathetic conversations, and shared meaning-making, leaders create environments where trust grows and performance accelerates. This isn't about enforcing compliance; it's about unlocking commitment.

In Chapter 5, we deepen the exploration of how aligned insights create adaptive cultures. We'll examine how leaders build psychological safety, foster inclusion, and design systems where values are lived daily, not just written on the wall. Where Chapter 4 equips you with the tools for alignment, Chapter 5 shows you how to sustain it when uncertainty, complexity, and pressure intensify.

"If alignment connects what we value with what we do, then culture is where those commitments come to life."

Chapter 5 explores how reflection becomes a cultural discipline rather than an individual act. We'll examine how organizations embed reflective practices into their rhythms, rituals, and systems to foster trust, belonging, and collective resilience. Moving beyond individual awareness, we'll explore how leaders cultivate spaces where teams can pause together, learn together, and adapt together, even in uncertainty.

CHAPTER 5

Reframing Resistance and Rebuilding Trust

Resistance is not defiance—it is data. It reveals where trust is thin, where meaning is missing, and where people need to be heard before they can move. This chapter explores how leaders can use resistance as a signal, rebuilding trust through empathy, dialogue, and adaptive action.

Learning Outcomes:

By the end of this chapter, you will be able to:

- Reframe resistance as a source of insight rather than opposition.
- Apply the Leadership Integration Model to diagnose trust gaps across roles.
- Use the Dual-Lens Framework to transform defensiveness into dialogue.
- Apply the Trust Diagnostic and Conversation Audit to restore alignment and safety.

Leadership Lens: When the Pace Feels Too Fast

You can't build trust at speed. You build it in the pause, when you slow down long enough to listen.

Nia tapped through the project dashboard on her tablet, watching the red flags multiply across rollout timelines. Several regions hadn't launched training yet, and tensions were rising. She pushed back a sigh as the indicators of strain became hard to ignore.

At the leadership alignment session, Marcus broke the silence: "We've been so focused on deliverables that I'm wondering whether we've really checked in on how people are doing. It's not resistance, they're overwhelmed."

Elena paused mid-sip of her coffee. "The board is asking for progress, but that kind of pressure without presence risks pushing people away instead of forward."

Instead of diving straight into solutions, Marcus pulled up the **Reflection Compass** on the screen and invited them to pause together:

- **Self**: "I'm feeling frustration, but curiosity might shift the tone."
- **Others**: "I notice confusion, not defiance, across the teams."
- **System**: "Different regions face unique challenges we haven't surfaced."
- **Purpose**: "Success demands adoption; adoption demands empathy."

That brief collective pause shifted the tone of the session. Rather than defending project timelines, the team collaboratively reengineered support structures, adjusted timelines, peer-support pairings, regional feedback loops. Progress didn't stall; it recalibrated.

What unfolded that day at WynnTech wasn't resistance for its own sake; it was a call for clarity. Behind each pushback was a signal about trust, communication, and psychological safety. Understanding those signals is the leader's first step toward rebuilding alignment.

WynnTech's pivot illustrates what recent research has confirmed: Reflective leadership practices aren't just soft skills—they're strategic capacities. To ground this in evidence, let's examine what current studies reveal about trust, psychological safety, and adaptive change.

Research Insight

This moment at WynnTech illustrates how reflective leadership, especially when embedded in team decision routines, builds high-performance cultures rooted in psychological safety, adaptation, and engagement.

Recent studies affirm that when leaders model and reinforce reflective practice:

- **On guided team reflexivity**: A recent study found that teams led by directive leaders showed significant improvement in performance when a guided team-reflexivity intervention was introduced over time (Santos et al. 2025).
- **On psychological safety**: Psychological safety enables employees to take interpersonal risks, such as asking questions, voicing dissent, or admitting mistakes, without fear of embarrassment or reprisal, and is foundational to innovation and transformation (Bonterre 2025; Edmondson and Kerrissey 2025).
- **On collective learning and the "slow down to speed up" approach**: Interrupting fast-paced execution with intentional pauses for reflection helps teams notice critical insights and realign direction, enabling long-term, sustainable performance (Santos et al. 2025).

This illustration underscores a shift: Reflection is no longer an individual discipline; it's becoming WynnTech's cultural practice. The slow pause is no longer a rare event but a system signal, enabling leaders at all levels to align purpose with empathy and performance with presence.

Here are three WynnTech-style micro-vignettes that deepen Chapter 5 by showing how resistance and trust-building play out across different leadership roles, project, change, and executive. Across WynnTech, resistance showed up in different ways depending on the role, and so did trust-building. These findings come to life when we look closer at how leaders across roles respond differently to resistance signals. At WynnTech, the interplay between project, change, and executive leadership revealed three distinct patterns. Here are three moments where leaders shifted their approach.

Micro-Vignette 1—Project Leader: Decoding Hidden Resistance

At WynnTech, Nia, the senior project leader, was rolling out a new workflow platform for the engineering division. The timeline was ambitious, and his weekly stand-ups were packed with progress updates.

Turning Point:

Despite clear technical plans, her team's tone in meetings was flat. Few people voiced concerns, yet deadlines kept slipping. Nia used the Trust Diagnostic (introduced later in this chapter) and discovered patterns: People didn't trust leadership's assurances about workload balance.

Leadership Action:

Instead of pushing harder, Nia held informal "coffee chats" with engineers in small groups. Through candid conversations, she uncovered fears about burnout and role redundancy. With this insight, she re-sequenced deliverables and created opt-in training for the new platform.

Impact:

Momentum improved not because pressure increased but because psychological safety grew. Nia learned that silence isn't always compliance; sometimes, it's the loudest form of resistance.

Micro-Vignette 2—Change Leader: Reframing Resistance as Care

Marcus, WynnTech's change lead, was responsible for employee engagement during a major restructuring. He faced a vocal group of supervisors skeptical about leadership's promises of "minimal disruption."

Turning Point:

Initially, Marcus interpreted the supervisors' pushback as resistance to change. But during a narrative inquiry session, he listened deeper. One supervisor said, "We're not against change; we just don't want our people blindsided again."

Leadership Action:

Marcus reframed his approach. He invited supervisors to co-create transition plans and incorporated their feedback into revised timelines. By giving them ownership, he shifted the energy from opposition to collaboration.

Impact:

Supervisors became champions for the restructuring, helping their teams process the uncertainty. Resistance turned out to be a signal of care, and trust was rebuilt through shared meaning-making.

Micro-Vignette 3—Executive Leader: Trust Through Transparency

WynnTech's CEO, Elena, was under pressure from the board to reduce operating costs. Rumors of layoffs were circulating, creating anxiety across the organization.

Turning Point:

Instead of letting uncertainty fester, Elena hosted a listening forum for employees. She openly acknowledged the difficult trade-offs ahead and shared her decision-making framework transparently.

Leadership Action:

She paired honesty with empathy: "We're exploring cost reductions, but we're also prioritizing retraining and redeployment wherever possible. I want you to hear that directly from me."

She also invited employees to anonymously submit questions, which were addressed in follow-up sessions.

Impact:

By naming the uncertainty, Elena prevented fear from morphing into rumor-fueled disengagement. Employees reported higher trust in leadership, even as restructuring plans continued.

By slowing down to listen beneath the surface, the WynnTech leadership team reframed resistance as a valuable data point rather than a threat. But gaining these insights consistently requires more than intuition; it calls for structured reflection. **The Trust Diagnostic and Conversation Audit** provides leaders with practical tools to uncover patterns of fear, hesitation, and misalignment before they escalate. These tools invite leaders to track trust-building behaviors, identify conversational blind spots, and turn moments of resistance into opportunities for shared sensemaking and adaptive action.

Tool: Trust Diagnostic and Conversation Audit

Identifying these patterns consistently requires more than intuition. To support leaders in tracking trust-building behaviors and conversational gaps, the **Trust Diagnostic and Conversation Audit** provides a structured approach to:

Assess Trust Levels—Provide guiding indicators (high, medium, low trust).

Audit Conversations—Track patterns where dissent, uncertainty, or concerns surface.

Action Insights—Help leaders see where engagement practices strengthen or erode trust.

Trust is the invisible currency of transformation. When it's present, conversations flow and collaboration thrives; when it's absent, resistance deepens beneath the surface. To move beyond assumptions, leaders need a way to make trust tangible. The **Trust Diagnostic and Conversation Audit** (Table 5.1) provides a simple framework to assess the current state of trust and reveal where dialogue is breaking down and where it can be strengthened.

Reflection in Action at WynnTech

While trust can be measured, it must also be lived. The WynnTech transformation highlights how reflective practices shift leadership behavior in real time (refer to Table 9.1). Each leader—project, change, and executive—encountered different signals of resistance. By applying the **Dual-Lens Framework** to these moments, they turned tension into alignment and resistance into renewed trust. The table below illustrates how reflective action unfolded across roles (Table 5.2).

Table 5.1 Trust diagnostic and conversation audit

Trust level	Observable signals	Conversational gaps	Leadership action insights
High trust	Teams volunteer dissent, share early warnings, and proactively offer solutions.	Few gaps, voices feel included, and tough issues surface naturally.	Reinforce openness: acknowledge contributions, celebrate transparency, and sustain feedback loops.
Moderate trust	Participation is inconsistent; some stakeholders hesitate while others dominate.	Missing voices signal "quiet resistance"; unspoken concerns persist beneath the surface.	Create safety: invite missing voices, normalize healthy dissent, and model curiosity over certainty.
Low trust	Teams avoid speaking up, resort to offline conversations, or default to compliance.	Conversations stall or fracture, hiding systemic issues until late in the process.	Rebuild foundations: name the trust gap, create structured listening forums, and act visibly on surfaced concerns.

Table 5.2 Reflection in action at WynnTech

Leadership role	Signals of resistance	Reflective insight (dual-lens)	Adaptive action
Project Leader—Nia	Frustration over shifting timelines; engineers missing stand-ups.	**Lens 1:** Feeling defensive. **Lens 2:** Engineers confused, not resistant.	Adds "context moments" to stand-ups; shares rationale behind milestones to rebuild clarity.
Change Leader—Marcus	Employee skepticism about training quality and new workflows.	**Lens 1:** Realizes his instinct is to "fix" fast. **Lens 2:** Learns skepticism signals care, not disengagement.	Hosts co-creation sessions for redesigning training paths with end users' input.
Executive Leader—Elena	Division leads bypass updates and raise concerns directly to the board.	**Lens 1:** Feels tension between defending the plan and hearing hard truths. **Lens 2:** Understands bypassing signals deeper trust gaps.	Hosts small-group forums with division heads; rebuilds alignment by reframing board updates as collective progress checks.

At WynnTech, this framework uncovered patterns leaders couldn't see on their own, allowing the team to address emerging trust gaps before they escalated.

Case in Progress: WynnTech's Trust Gap

The WynnTech transformation team had just wrapped a leadership review when tensions began to surface. A new enterprise resource planning (ERP) system was being rolled out, intended to unify workflows across three divisions.

In a leadership sync, Marcus, the change leader, noticed Elena, the executive sponsor, receiving increasingly direct pushback from team leads. One project manager said:

"We're working overtime to meet deadlines, but no one's asking what's breaking down on the ground."

Instead of defending the program timelines, Marcus paused and leaned into curiosity. Using insights from the Trust Diagnostic, he recognized a deeper signal: This wasn't defiance—it was fear of being unheard.

Elena decided to call a cross-functional session. Nia, the senior project lead, set up feedback sessions where frontline staff could voice concerns about training gaps and usability without repercussion. Over several weeks, the leadership team captured recurring patterns of resistance and used them to adjust rollout milestones and co-create revised communication plans.

Trust didn't rebuild overnight, but, by treating resistance as a message, WynnTech shifted from defensive leadership to collaborative problem-solving. Recognizing patterns is the first step; responding effectively requires leaders to pause and examine both their internal reactions and their external communication choices.

Practice-in-Action Exercise

In your next leadership meeting, pause agenda progress and ask: What concerns are we not hearing right now? Track insights in your diagnostic tool.

Beyond individual reflection, collective dialogue accelerates alignment. Hosting this conversation with your team helps surface unspoken fears and create shared clarity.

Host This Conversation

- **"Where have we misread resistance as defiance rather than care?"**
- **"What conversations are happening outside the room that should be happening inside it?"**

Trust requires ongoing intention. This commitment statement invites leaders to shift from controlling resistance to co-creating alignment.

Chapter Close: From Resistance to Shared Meaning

Chapter 5 laid the foundation for decoding resistance and rebuilding trust. We explored how trust is both fragile and actionable, shaped by how leaders invite dissent, respond to uncertainty, and honor what sits beneath surface tensions.

Chapter 6, Making Sense Together: Storytelling, Listening, and Dialogic Leadership, takes the next step. Trust deepens when leaders create space for collective meaning-making. Here, we move beyond decoding resistance to engaging diverse voices, surfacing hidden stories, and co-creating alignment.

Through storytelling, listening, and dialogic practices, leaders turn fragmented conversations into coherent narratives that connect purpose with action. When leaders listen not to defend or reply, but to understand the story beneath the surface, they open the door to transformation. Making sense together is how organizations find clarity and move forward, even when complexity threatens to divide.

CHAPTER 6

Making Sense Together: Storytelling, Listening, and Dialogue

Storytelling and dialogue are how people make sense of change. In moments of uncertainty, the stories leaders tell, and how they listen, determine whether transformation feels imposed or shared. This chapter explores how meaning is co-created through conversation and how listening becomes a leadership practice that builds belonging and clarity.

Learning Outcomes:

By the end of this chapter, you will be able to:

- Explain how narrative and dialogue shape shared meaning in transformation.
- Apply the Leadership Integration Model to foster cross-role coherence through story.
- Use the Dual-Lens Framework to listen reflectively and facilitate sensemaking conversations.
- Apply the Reflective Dialogue Guide to turn discussion into alignment and action.

Leadership Lens—Finding Meaning in the Noise

The cross-functional workshop was supposed to accelerate delivery; instead, it exposed competing priorities and buried assumptions. Yet, within the chaos, a path toward alignment began to emerge.

The conference room at WynnTech felt heavy with unspoken tension. It was the third cross-functional dialogue workshop since the transformation began, and Marcus had learned by now that the real insights surfaced only when people felt safe enough to speak.

He dimmed the overhead lights slightly, adjusted the chairs into an informal setting, and began quietly:

"One word. That's all I want to start with. How are you feeling about where we are right now?"

There was a pause, the kind that stretches longer than anyone expects. Then, one by one:

"Exhausted."

"Hopeful."

"Skeptical."

"Committed."

As each voice entered the space, the atmosphere shifted. Shoulders relaxed. A few people leaned forward. Marcus noticed Priya from Engineering biting her lip before she added:

"Honestly? I'm confused. We keep talking about agility, but I don't understand how my team fits into the bigger picture."

Her admission broke the dam. For the next 20 minutes, the conversation unfolded into stories, moments of frustration, small victories, and fears about the future. By the time they finished, the room felt different.

No data point, survey, or dashboard could have created this shift. Stories had done what numbers couldn't:

- Revealed the emotional undercurrents shaping decisions.
- Surfaced hidden connections between teams.
- Built a fragile but growing sense of trust.

As the session closed, Marcus scribbled a note into his tablet:

"Change doesn't fail because of resistance. It fails when we don't make meaning together."

Storytelling had turned silence into dialogue, uncertainty into connection. For the first time in weeks, WynnTech's cross-functional leaders left not just informed but also understood.

The experiences in WynnTech's dialogue session illustrate a deeper truth: Transformation doesn't just rely on data or dashboards. To move forward together, leaders must help people make sense of uncertainty. This is where storytelling, listening, and reflective dialogue come in. These moments at WynnTech underscore a larger truth: To navigate transformation effectively, leaders must create meaning together. This sets the stage for understanding why storytelling, dialogue, and listening matter so deeply.

At WynnTech, the shift was not from strategy to story but from telling people what to do to inviting them into what they were building together. The leaders realized that alignment only endures when people see themselves in the story of change.

Core Concepts and Framing: Storytelling, Listening, and Dialogue as Sensemaking Practices

Transformation doesn't emerge from data dashboards—it comes to life through shared stories, deep listening, and intentional dialogue. This chapter invites leaders to shift from delivering reports to curating meaning, from commanding direction to fostering conversation.

Story as Sensemaking

Complex change often leads to confusion, even when information is abundant. Sensemaking, a term coined by organizational theorist Karl Weick (1995), describes the process of creating coherent meaning from ambiguity. It's not passive reporting; it's active interpretation. In narrative terms, story is how we make sense of uncertainty, aligning experiences and memory through language. In Weick's (1995) words, organizations engage in sensemaking as "ongoing retrospective development of plausible images that rationalize what people are doing."

Without story, numeric data lack emotional traction; without narrative, direction lacks connection. Storytelling allows leaders and teams to draw meaning from ambiguity, connect across silos, and build shared understanding.

Dialogue as Leadership

Story isn't effective when delivered monologue-style. Reflection deepens when paired with dialogue, a leadership practice where listening, suspending judgment, honoring voices, and voicing authentic presence converge. In systems thinking terms, this is dialogic leadership. It moves beyond exchanging viewpoints to generating emergent insights that reshape perception and action (Bushe and Marshak 2016).

Dialogue creates the conditions for psychological safety: People feel heard, and stories can surface without fear. This establishes the relational foundation for collaboration, creativity, and trust.

Understanding the "why" behind storytelling and dialogue is only the first step. The next is seeing how these practices translate into the distinct responsibilities of project leaders, change leaders, and executive leaders within the Leadership Integration Model. Understanding the role of storytelling is one thing; applying it within specific leadership responsibilities is another.

In Chapter 5, we learned to listen beneath resistance to find the trust gaps within systems. This chapter extends that practice by focusing on how leaders create meaning once trust is rebuilt. Storytelling and dialogue are how organizations learn aloud—they translate reflection and alignment into shared understanding.

Why Story Matters in Transformation

Stories are sensemaking tools; they connect logic and emotion, and data and belief. In complex change, a good story does not simplify reality but creates a map people can navigate together.

Storytelling, Listening, and the Leadership Integration Model

The Leadership Integration Model (presented in earlier chapters) finds durable expression in dialogic practices:

- **Project Leaders** anchor story in the everyday work, eliciting insights from team members to ground updates in lived experience.

- **Change Leaders** use narrative tools not just for messaging but also to surface emotional energy and reframe resistance into meaning.
- **Executive Leaders** model presence by entering dialogue sessions as listeners first, demonstrating openness, curiosity, and reflexive leadership.

Together, storytelling and dialogue (Denning 2005) help leaders create shared meaning, so teams move not just in parallel but in resonance.

To bring these leadership practices to life, let me introduce the **Reflective Dialogue Guide**, a framework designed to help leaders facilitate story-based conversations that reveal hidden dynamics and foster shared meaning. This guide introduces the foundational steps leaders can use to host story-based conversations that surface meaning, deepen trust, and foster connection.

Reflective Dialogue Guide

In complex transformations, dialogue isn't just about exchanging information; it's about creating shared meaning. Storytelling gives people a way to surface experiences, while deep listening allows leaders to uncover the patterns, fears, and aspirations beneath the surface.

This guide helps leaders and teams structure reflective dialogues that foster connection, build trust, and generate insights that data alone cannot reveal. Whether used in project stand-ups, cross-functional sessions, or executive retreats, these steps (visible in Table 6.1 below) create space for voices to be heard and meaning to emerge.

Why This Matters

Research on sensemaking in complex systems highlights that collective understanding emerges when leaders create spaces where stories, perspectives, and emotional realities can intersect (Weick 1995; Maitlis and Christianson 2014). In practice, this means leaders must balance listening deeply when guiding toward purpose, cultivating environments where trust and collaboration thrive.

Table 6.1 Reflective dialogue guide

Step	Purpose	Example prompts/ practices	Leadership application
1. **Open with Story**	Invite personal experiences to surface meaning and emotion.	"Share one moment that captures how you're feeling about this change."	Builds empathy and frames transformation as a shared journey.
2. **Listen to Understand**	Suspend judgment to hear what's beneath the words.	"What matters most to you about what's changing?"	Creates psychological safety and invites honesty.
3. **Notice Shared Themes**	Surface patterns, hopes, and concerns emerging across stories.	"I'm hearing three recurring threads across our experiences…"	Links individual meaning to collective insight.
4. **Connect to Purpose**	Anchor reflections in shared vision and values.	"How does this connect to what we're trying to achieve together?"	Reaffirms alignment and builds confidence.
5. **Move Toward Action**	Translate insights into next steps while maintaining inclusivity.	"What's one small change we can make based on what we've heard?"	Turns dialogue into co-created solutions, not top-down mandates.

The value of this guide becomes clearer when applied in real-world contexts. At WynnTech, Marcus used this framework to create space for voices, uncover shared challenges, and strengthen trust across functions.

Case in Point: Bridging Silos Through Story at WynnTech

The customer success and engineering teams had been clashing for weeks over delays in a new feature rollout. Frustrations simmered under the surface, spilling into curt emails and fragmented conversations. Elena, the Executive Leader, called a special alignment session. Instead of launching into status updates, she began with a pause:

"Before we talk timelines, I want to understand where each of you is right now. One word, how are you showing up today?"

Responses trickled in:

"Exhausted."

"Defensive."

"Curious."

"Determined."

Elena captured each word on the whiteboard without judgment. Then, using the **Reflective Dialogue Guide**, she shifted the session from problem-solving to story-sharing:

- **Open with Story**: "Can someone share a moment this week that shows how this rollout is impacting your work?"
  A customer success manager described a call where a long-time client felt "kept in the dark."
- **Listen to Understand**: Instead of reacting, Elena asked: "What made that moment so hard for you?"
- **Notice Shared Themes**: Across multiple stories, two clear patterns emerged—teams lacked a single source of truth and felt blindsided by late-stage changes.
- **Connect to Purpose**: Elena reframed the frustration: "If our goal is client trust, these stories are gold. They show us where the gaps are."
- **Move Toward Action**: Together, they designed a cross-team communication channel and agreed on joint client touchpoints before major feature launches.

By the end of the session, energy had shifted from blame to collaboration. What began as siloed frustrations became collective sensemaking, where each voice reshaped the narrative of change.

The WynnTech dialogue session illustrates the power of collective sensemaking: When leaders create intentional space for story, listening, and shared meaning, transformation shifts from something delivered to something co-created. But these outcomes don't happen by chance. They emerge when leaders deliberately cultivate practices that slow the conversation down, surface lived experiences, and connect individual narratives back to a shared purpose.

In the sections that follow, we explore reflective dialogue as a leadership discipline, introducing tools and prompts that help leaders facilitate richer conversations, decode resistance, and weave alignment across diverse voices. By combining structured frameworks with authentic listening, leaders can transform uncertainty into clarity and trust.

While the WynnTech story demonstrates what reflective dialogue can achieve, leaders can begin by using the following prompts to integrate these practices into their own conversations.

Conversation Reflection Prompts

These prompts are designed to integrate **Lens 1** (internal experience) and **Lens 2** (external conversation) into the practice of sensemaking through storytelling and dialogue:

Lens 1—Internal Experience

- What story am I telling myself about this change, and how does it shape how I listen?
- Where do my assumptions or fears limit my ability to hear others fully?
- How does my personal purpose connect to the collective purpose we're working toward?

Lens 2—External Conversation

- What shared narratives exist within this team or organization? How are they helping or hindering transformation?
- Whose stories are shaping our decisions, and whose voices are missing?
- How can I create space where divergent perspectives can coexist without collapsing into conflict?

For a structured tool to host effective storytelling and listening sessions, see the Reflective Dialogue Guide in Appendix E.

WynnTech Case—Making Sense Together

The WynnTech transformation team had reached a breaking point. Months of shifting priorities and conflicting messages had left employees frustrated and disengaged. To rebuild trust, Marcus (Change Leader) convened a cross-functional storytelling session using the Reflective Dialogue Guide.

He began by setting the intention:

"We're here to make sense of what this transformation means to us, together. There are no wrong stories."

One by one, participants shared brief stories about their recent experiences:

- A project lead described staying late three nights in a row because timelines were unclear.
- A frontline customer specialist spoke about the fear of losing client relationships during the platform migration.
- An IT engineer expressed pride in solving a critical integration issue no one else could untangle.

As people spoke, others listened, really listened. Patterns emerged: frustration with misaligned priorities, pride in small wins, and shared anxiety about job security. Elena (Executive Leader) remained silent for most of the session, simply listening. When she finally spoke, she said:

"I didn't realize how much uncertainty we've created in your roles. I hear you, and we need to fix this, together."

The tone of the group shifted. For the first time in months, there was a sense of being seen, not as roles but as people contributing to a shared journey.

These reflective practices aren't just helpful; they're backed by research. Scholars like Karl Weick (1995) and Amy Edmondson (2019) emphasize that collective sensemaking and psychological safety are essential for navigating ambiguity and driving transformation. The outcomes at WynnTech reflect what research consistently shows about sensemaking in complex systems.

Storytelling, Listening, and Collective Sensemaking

In complex transformations, meaning isn't delivered through slide decks or dashboards—it's co-created in the conversations between people. Storytelling, active listening, and reflective dialogue are not "soft" skills; they are strategic tools for navigating ambiguity. Research shows that when leaders intentionally create spaces for people to share their lived experiences, organizations surface deeper insights and foster stronger alignment across silos (Weick et al. 2005).

At WynnTech, the storytelling session revealed unspoken fears, uncelebrated wins, and systemic blind spots. These insights wouldn't have surfaced through surveys or metrics alone. By inviting multiple voices into the sensemaking process, Marcus, Nia, and Elena modeled a shift from managing change to meaning-making within change, a critical leadership competency in today's adaptive environments (Snowden and Boone 2007).

Reflective dialogue builds collective intelligence by weaving together individual perspectives into shared understanding. It transforms resistance into insight and confusion into connection. Leaders who practice this consistently position their organizations to adapt faster and innovate more effectively (Edmondson 2019).

To move from insight to application, this exercise provides a simple structure for introducing reflective dialogue into your next team setting.

Practice-in-Action Exercise

In your next team dialogue, invite participants to share a recent moment that made them proud or uncertain about the change journey. Use the Reflective Dialogue Guide to structure the conversation and notice where meaning emerges beyond metrics.

Equally important is equipping yourself to open up these conversations. Use the prompts below to invite richer discussion and ensure all voices are heard.

Host This Conversation

- **"How can storytelling make space for voices that aren't usually heard?"**
- **"What would change if our meetings began with meaning, not metrics?"**

Chapter Close: Making Meaning Together

In transformation, data only informs, but it is stories that connect. Facts alone rarely shift mindsets or build trust. What moves people is hearing themselves reflected in a larger narrative, where their experiences and emotions are acknowledged and woven into a shared purpose.

By hosting reflective dialogue and listening deeply, leaders create the conditions for sensemaking, the space where uncertainty is transformed into collective insight. Through storytelling, leaders and teams begin to see patterns, uncover hidden dynamics, and find language for challenges they couldn't name before. These conversations become bridges: between individuals and the system, between what's known and what's emerging.

At WynnTech, we saw how this worked in practice. Once leaders shifted from defending the plan to inviting diverse stories about the transformation, they unlocked new possibilities. Instead of managing resistance, they began decoding its meaning. Trust deepened, and alignment strengthened, not because differences disappeared but because they were seen and heard.

This chapter highlighted how storytelling and listening are not soft skills; they are strategic tools for navigating complexity. When leaders invite story into the room, they don't just gather information; they generate connection, empathy, and momentum.

In Chapter 7, we take the next step: exploring how these narratives and conversations can be scaled across systems. We'll look at how leaders move beyond individual meaning-making to create organizational coherence, where stories, strategy, and structure align to drive transformation.

PART 3

Leading from the Edge

Framework Preview

Part 3 brings the two frameworks together in full. Structural coherence and reflective presence merge into a single practice of people-centered transformation. At **WynnTech**, the lessons learned through conflict, dialogue, and reflection mature into an integrated way of leading, where systems and relationships evolve together. The *Leadership Integration Model* provides the architecture; the *Dual-Lens Framework* keeps it human, adaptive, and alive.

CHAPTER 7

Modeling the Change You Seek

Transformation takes root when leaders embody the values they ask others to follow. This chapter explores modeling as the visible bridge between intention and impact—how presence, integrity, and consistency shape culture more powerfully than policy.

Learning Outcomes:

By the end of this chapter, you will be able to:

- Explain why modeling behavior is the foundation of cultural change.
- Apply the Leadership Integration Model to demonstrate alignment across roles.
- Use the Dual-Lens Framework to stay authentic under pressure and connect inner values to outer actions.
- Apply the Alignment Arc and Leadership Signals Map to make consistency visible across systems.

Leadership Lens: Who Gets a Seat at the Table

The room fell silent when the question was asked: "Whose voices are missing?" Suddenly, transformation wasn't just about structure and systems; it was about belonging.

Elena stood at the front of the glass-walled conference room, facing her senior leadership team. The quarterly transformation review was supposed to focus on metrics, but her voice carried a different weight today.

"I need to name something I missed," she began, unclasping her hands. "When I pushed the restructuring decision through last month, I didn't fully listen. I can see now the impact that had, on trust, on morale, and on our ability to move forward together."

The room was quiet. Not the kind of silence that signals judgment or discomfort but a collective pause. Around the table, heads lifted. Some exchanged glances; others leaned back, visibly letting go of tension.

"I can't ask you to model collaboration," Elena continued, "if I'm not living it myself. That changes today."

In that moment, she wasn't just giving direction. She was signaling values, vulnerability, accountability, and alignment between words and actions. Her presence set the tone for the culture WynnTech aspired to build: a place where modeling change mattered as much as managing it.

In that moment, Elena's willingness to name her oversight re-framed what leadership looks like during transformation. Modeling change isn't about perfection; it's about alignment. When leaders demonstrate the same vulnerability, curiosity, and accountability they ask of others, they create powerful cultural signals. These moments set the stage for deeper trust and engagement, which are essential when navigating uncertainty.

The WynnTech team had heard a hundred messages about change, but what mattered was what they saw. When Elena chose to admit a misstep in front of her leaders, the room shifted. It wasn't a speech that restored trust; it was modeling.

Chapter 6 showed how dialogue creates shared meaning. Chapter 7 turns that meaning into movement, when leaders model the behaviors they want to see. Consistency between message and action is the truest form of communication.

Why Modeling Matters

People watch leaders more than they listen to them. Research on transformational and inclusive leadership shows that trust and psychological safety grow when leaders demonstrate humility, accountability, and follow-through. Culture isn't declared; it's demonstrated.

The following section explores why behavior becomes the strongest form of communication and how modeling the change you seek shapes culture more effectively than any strategic plan.

Core Concepts and Framing: Modeling the Change You Seek

Transformation isn't a strategy—it's a signal. What leaders do, not just what they say, reverberates through teams. Modeling the change you want to see becomes a powerful way to communicate values, build trust, and reshape norms.

Values-Based Leadership and Modeling Behavior

Research on values-based leadership shows that authentic, consistent behavior helps build cultures grounded in integrity and alignment. As leadership scholar Harry Kraemer (2025) advises, "self-reflection and clear value alignment" are essential to sustain meaningful leadership through change. Similarly, *Harvard Business Review* consultant Craig Dickerson (2025) positions values-based leadership as rooted in emotional awareness—your ability to recognize triggers and intentionally respond from purpose, not reactivity. When leaders' actions align with expressed values, followers are more likely to trust, follow, and adopt similar practices. This isn't about perfection; it's about reflective integrity.

Presence Under Pressure

Modeling change is most visible when things go wrong. The Dual-Lens Framework helps leaders stay centered:

- Lens 1—Internal Experience: Notice defensiveness and return to values before responding.
- Lens 2—External Conversation: Acknowledge impact openly and invite collaboration on next steps.

Every crisis becomes an opportunity to signal authenticity and psychological safety.

Modeling Builds Psychological Safety

Amy Edmondson's (2019) pioneering work illustrates that team learning and innovation flourish not because uncertainty vanishes but because leaders model transparency and accountability in the face of uncertainty. When leaders act vulnerably and own their mistakes, they create space for others to engage, experiment, and grow.

Modeling Shapes Behavior Through Social Learning

Social learning theory demonstrates that people learn not only from formal instruction but also by observing behavior. Leaders serve as models: When team members see behaviors being rewarded or tolerated, they adopt them, whether high trust or duplicity. Modeling is often more persuasive than any message.

Linking to the Dual-Lens Framework and Leadership Integration Model

- **Lens 1—Internal Experience**: Being clear that my behaviors are aligned with my values isn't just ethical; it's strategic. It moves tension from "what's being asked" to "who we are becoming."
- **Lens 2—External Signals**: Teams gauge priorities not by what's said but by what's modeled. When leaders embody values like curiosity or humility, they cascade into shared expectation.

Within the **Leadership Integration Model**, modeling behavior matters at every level:

- **Project leaders** like Nia reinforce adaptability by modeling learning, not just delivery.
- **Change leaders** such as Marcus invite narrative learning by incorporating their own developmental stories.
- **Executives** like Elena redirect culture by showing vulnerability and setting norms through personal behavior.

Leadership Signals Map

In times of transformation, leaders shape culture less by what they say and more by what they do. Every action, or inaction, sends a signal about what truly matters. The Leadership Signals Map (Table 7.1) helps leaders intentionally connect their desired cultural values to visible daily behaviors. When values are embodied consistently, they create clarity, trust, and alignment across the organization.

This table does three things:

1. Introduces that connecting values clearly, and ties it back to transformation and culture.
2. Provides a ready-to-use table leaders can immediately apply in their teams.
3. Connects back to the Dual-Lens Framework through reflection and conversation prompts.

Table 7.1 Leadership signals map

Desired cultural belief	Leadership behaviors that signal it	Potential mixed signals to avoid	Conversation prompts for alignment
Psychological safety	Admits mistakes openly; invites dissenting views	Punishes failure or disagreement	"What would make it easier to speak up without fear?"
Collaboration over silos	Models cross-team decision-making; shares credit broadly	Hoards information; rewards individual wins only	"Where can we create more shared accountability?"
Continuous learning	Reflects publicly on personal growth; seeks feedback regularly	Defends status quo; avoids vulnerability	"What's one thing I've learned this month I can share with you?"
Accountability with empathy	Holds self and others to commitments while considering constraints	Over-indexes on control or ignores follow-through	"How do we balance care and clarity in setting expectations?"
Inclusivity and belonging	Seeks diverse voices in decision-making; celebrates different perspectives	Defaults to "usual voices" in critical conversations	"Whose perspective hasn't been heard yet?"

Modeling change isn't only about big declarations; it's lived in small, everyday signals. The choices you make, the conversations you hold, and even the silences you allow all shape how others experience your leadership. The **Leadership Signals Map** offers one way to see those patterns, but, to truly shift them, you need to reflect on both your inner drivers and the external messages you send.

That's where the dual-lens reflection comes in, inviting you to look inward at your intentions while also considering how your actions are interpreted by others.

Dual-Lens Reflection Prompt

Use this prompt to explore how your behaviors signal beliefs during change:

Lens 1—Internal Experience

- Where might there be gaps between the values I say I hold and the behaviors I model?
- What fears or habits might be driving unintentional signals?

Lens 2—External Conversation

- What messages are my actions sending to my team and stakeholders right now?
- How could I use intentional storytelling or behavior shifts to make our desired culture more visible?

Reflection is the first step, but modeling change truly takes shape in dialogue. Once you've examined your intentions and actions through the Dual-Lens Framework, the next step is to bring these insights into your conversations. These prompts are designed to help you transform private reflection into shared understanding, aligning personal values with collective purpose.

Insight without experimentation rarely drives transformation. Once you've reflected on what your actions communicate and surfaced these themes in dialogue, the next step is to translate awareness into daily practice. This exercise is designed to help you intentionally test small shifts in your behavior, modeling the culture you want to create and inviting others to do the same.

Host This Conversation

Bring your leadership team or project group together and invite discussion around these questions:

- **"What behaviors signal our real priorities as a team or organization?"**
- **"Where might there be gaps between what we say matters and what we actually model?"**
- **"How can we hold each other accountable for leading by example?"**

Encourage openness and psychological safety by modeling vulnerability yourself, for example, by naming one behavior you're currently working on.

Awareness is only the beginning. Modeling the change you seek requires turning reflection into intentional action and then inviting others into shared meaning-making. The following tools and prompts guide you from personal alignment to collective accountability.

Practice-in-Action Exercise—Modeling the Values You Seek

Step 1. Identify: Choose one behavior you want to shift so it better reflects the culture you're advocating.

Step 2. Practice: Commit to one week of consistent action, whether pausing to listen before responding, sharing personal uncertainties, or making time to recognize contributions.

Step 3. Invite Feedback: Ask a peer, mentor, or team member to observe your behavior and share what cultural signals they perceive.

Step 4. Reflect: At week's end, journal about what shifted in your presence, team dynamics, and trust levels.

Personal reflection and individual commitments are powerful, but lasting cultural change happens when these conversations extend beyond ourselves. Hosting intentional dialogue with your team creates shared understanding and collective accountability. These prompts are designed to help teams surface assumptions, clarify values, and co-create behaviors that model the change together.

Reflecting, practicing, and engaging in dialogue create the groundwork for alignment, but lasting transformation requires a personal declaration. By articulating a clear commitment, leaders turn intention into accountability, signaling to themselves and others that their behaviors will consistently reflect the values they want to see.

Chapter Close: Inspiring Trust Through Presence

Modeling the change you seek is about embodying values in action, becoming the clearest cultural signal your team has. When leaders demonstrate alignment between their words and behaviors, they inspire trust and create a foundation where others feel safe to follow.

In Chapter 8, *Making Sense Together: Storytelling, Listening, and Dialogue*, we expand on this foundation by exploring how collective narratives emerge and why shared meaning-making is essential in complex transformations. If behavior signals what matters, story connects us to why it matters and invites everyone to shape the journey together.

CHAPTER 8

Learning at the Edge: Vulnerability and Growth in Leadership

Growth happens at the edge of comfort. This chapter explores how vulnerability becomes a source of strength and how leaders cultivate learning cultures that embrace uncertainty, experimentation, and reflection. When leaders show they are still learning, they give permission for others to do the same.

Learning Outcomes:

By the end of this chapter, you will be able to:

- Describe the relationship between vulnerability, learning, and adaptive leadership.
- Apply the Leadership Integration Model to create psychologically safe learning environments.
- Use the Dual-Lens Framework to navigate the discomfort of growth with intention.
- Apply the Growth Zone Reflection Matrix to help teams and individuals move from fear to curiosity.

Leadership Lens: The Spiral of Uncertainty

Deadlines shifted again, priorities collided, and confusion spread faster than updates could keep up. Leaders were forced to confront their own discomfort with ambiguity and lean into adaptive practice.

Nia stared at the proposal draft, her fingers hovering above the keyboard. Every sentence felt fragile, as though one misplaced word could unravel the entire pitch. Across the table, Marcus was unusually quiet, reflecting on a story he'd shared during their last team session, a vulnerable admission about how the emotional weight of leading change was catching up with him.

Later that afternoon, Elena noticed Nia lingering after their leadership huddle.

"You seem distracted," Elena said softly.

"I just..." Nia hesitated. "I don't feel certain about any of this."

Elena nodded, pulling out a chair. "That's where growth starts. When certainty slips, curiosity takes its place."

In that moment, Nia realized she wasn't being asked to be perfect, she was being invited to lead from her edge.

Nia's experience reflects a truth many leaders overlook: Growth rarely happens in comfort. It emerges at the threshold between what we know and what stretches us, a space where vulnerability, reflection, and courage meet.

At WynnTech, the team had learned to talk more honestly about mistakes, but vulnerability was still rare in public. When Nia shared that she was uncertain about the next project phase, silence followed, then relief. The conversation shifted from blame to learning.

Chapter 7 showed how leaders model integrity through visible action. Chapter 8 moves deeper into *inner modeling*: showing not certainty but learning in motion. Vulnerability is the practice that transforms reflection into growth.

Why Growth Requires Discomfort

Leaders cannot develop new capacity without encountering the unknown. The Dual-Lens Framework helps make this productive:

- *Lens 1—Internal Experience:* Notice fear or ego reactions when feedback or change feels threatening.

- *Lens 2—External Conversation:* Name vulnerability as part of learning; invite others to share what you're testing or unsure about.

Core Concepts and Framing

In today's complex, uncertain environments, leaders are constantly confronted with situations where they don't have all the answers. Far from signaling weakness, vulnerability is the entry point to authentic leadership growth.

Key ideas worth highlighting:

- **Vulnerability as Strength**
  Brené Brown (2018) argues that vulnerability is not about exposure for its own sake but about building trust and connection by showing up authentically.
- **Discomfort as a Growth Signal**
  Stepping into stretch zones, where discomfort signals possibility, not threat, and activates deeper learning and creativity.
- **Leadership as Adaptive Learning**
  Amy Edmondson's (2019) work on psychological safety underscores that when leaders model openness, they normalize uncertainty, enabling teams to experiment, learn, and adapt together.

Leadership isn't about knowing everything. It's about creating the conditions where collective learning thrives.

Reflection Prompts

Recognizing where we stand on the growth edge is just the beginning. True transformation comes when leaders intentionally connect their internal experience with the external signals they send to others. The dual-lens reflection prompts below (Table 8.1) creates that bridge.

These prompts support leaders in integrating self-awareness with relational awareness, encouraging alignment between personal growth and team culture.

Table 8.1 Dual-lens conversation reflection prompts

Lens	Reflective prompts
Lens 1—Internal experience	What discomfort am I currently avoiding, and why? How has vulnerability shaped my leadership journey so far?
Lens 2—External conversation	When have I created space for others to share openly, even when it was hard to hear? How can I use my story to normalize uncertainty and model growth?

Leaders often believe that growth comes from expertise, from already knowing what to do. Yet in transformation, growth comes from leaning into the edges of discomfort. The Growth Zone Reflection Matrix that follows, helps leaders locate where they currently stand and where deliberate stretching will foster personal and organizational transformation. By identifying whether you're in a comfort, stretch, or stress zone, you can make intentional choices about how to grow while modeling the vulnerability needed for others to follow.

Case in Progress: WynnTech Stretching into Growth

In a leadership session at WynnTech, Nia admitted she had been hesitating to present a new project proposal because she feared it wouldn't meet shifting priorities. "I keep telling myself I'm prepared," she said, "but honestly, I'm not sure where the goalposts are anymore."

Marcus nodded. He'd been facilitating more employee forums than ever and felt drained by the emotional labor of holding so many perspectives at once. Elena, listening quietly, leaned forward. "I've realized something," she said. "We've been asking everyone to stretch, but I haven't modeled my own discomfort. So, here's mine." She then shared her uncertainty about executive-level decisions still unresolved.

In that moment, the tension in the room shifted. By naming their own stretch zones, each leader modeled a willingness to learn at the edge (see Table 8.2 below). Trust deepened, and others felt safer admitting where they, too, were still growing.

Once leaders locate themselves within the matrix, the next step is to make meaning of that awareness. Using the Dual-Lens Framework,

Table 8.2 Aligning with the growth zone reflection matrix

Leader	Comfort zone	Stretch zone	Stress zone	Key learning edge
Nia (*Project Leader*)	Familiar workflows and previous project frameworks	Drafting new proposals amid shifting priorities	Feeling stuck if expectations remain unclear	Building confidence in ambiguity
Marcus (*Change Leader*)	Facilitating known forums with set agendas	Hosting emotionally complex dialogues across teams	Risk of burnout from constant sensemaking	Balancing empathy with personal capacity
Elena (*Executive Leader*)	Delivering confident directives from the top	Publicly naming her own uncertainties and incomplete decisions	Potential credibility concerns if vulnerability is misunderstood	Modeling openness to normalize discomfort

these reflection prompts encourage you to consider both your internal experiences (Lens 1) and your external signals and conversations (Lens 2).

Conversation Reflection Prompts

Lens 1—Internal Experience

- "What discomfort am I currently avoiding?"
- "How has vulnerability shaped my leadership path?"

Lens 2—External Conversations

- "When have I made it safe for others to share openly?"
- "How can I use my story to normalize uncertainty and growth?"

Reflection builds insight, but it is deliberate action that turns insight into leadership practice. The following exercise offers a simple, practical way to step into your stretch zone.

Practice-in-Action Exercise

In your next team meeting, share a personal moment when you felt uncertain or unprepared and what you learned from it. Then, invite your team members to do the same.

By modeling openness, leaders normalize growth and cultivate a collective willingness to embrace discomfort. Sometimes, leadership isn't about providing answers but creating space for dialogue that surfaces unspoken truths. Use these conversation starters to deepen trust and understanding.

Host This Conversation

- **"What does it mean to lead from the edge of your comfort zone?"**
- **"Where are we asking others to grow without modeling that same courage ourselves?"**
- **"How might we better support each other as we stretch into uncertainty?"**

Leadership growth is sustained when reflection, dialogue, and practice culminate in personal commitment. The statement below invites leaders to anchor their growth journey in intention. Moments of stretch and discomfort aren't obstacles to transformation—they're the path. By leaning into vulnerability and modeling growth, leaders signal that learning is not just accepted but expected.

Chapter Close: Embracing Discomfort

Leadership at the edge isn't just about personal growth; it sets the tone for how organizations adapt to profound shifts. In Chapter 8, we explored how vulnerability and stretch become catalysts for learning. But what happens when transformation isn't just cultural, when it's technological, systemic, and reshaping how people experience work itself?

Chapter 9 takes us into the realities of digital transformation, where technology often takes center stage, yet people remain the linchpin of success. We'll explore how to keep humanity, empathy, and inclusion at the heart of technological change while using the Dual-Lens Framework to balance human experience with strategic execution.

PART 4

Embedding Systemic Change

Framework Preview

Part 4 brings the story and the frameworks to their point of integration. At *Wynn Tech*, the lessons from alignment, trust, and learning evolve into an enduring way of leading, where presence and structure reinforce one another. The ***Leadership Integration Model*** provides continuity of roles and accountability; the ***Dual-Lens Framework*** sustains reflective awareness and connection. Together, they form the practice of people-centered transformation that continues beyond the project itself.

CHAPTER 9

Centering People in Digital Transformation

Digital transformation is never just technological—it's human. Systems change only when the people who design, use, and are affected by them feel seen and included. This chapter reframes technology projects as people-centered change initiatives that integrate empathy, ethics, and learning.

Learning Outcomes:

By the end of this chapter, you will be able to:

- Explain why digital transformation succeeds or fails based on people, not platforms.
- Apply the Leadership Integration Model to align human experience with technological design.
- Use the Dual-Lens Framework to translate data into dialogue and insight.
- Apply the Reflective Compass Map to evaluate how digital shifts affect culture and trust.

Leadership Lens: Holding the Center

Momentum was slipping. Pressure mounted to declare victory and move on, but the leaders sensed that rushing now would unravel everything they'd built.

The hum of laptops filled the project room as the WynnTech digital rollout team gathered for their weekly check-in. Screens displayed timelines, milestones, and adoption metrics. Yet something wasn't clicking.

"I don't get it," said Shelton, one of the lead developers, pushing his chair back. "We built everything exactly to spec, but no one's using the new platform."

Across the table, Marcus leaned forward. "Because it's not about the platform," he said quietly. "It's about trust."

Elena, who had joined the session as part of her new commitment to "listen first," nodded. "We designed for efficiency," she said, "but we forgot to design for people."

Silence followed, not defensive, but reflective. In that pause, the team realized that the success of their digital transformation hinged less on the code they'd written and more on the conversations they hadn't yet had.

Human experience, emotional trust, and collaborative ownership must sit at the center of digital transformation. This wasn't about fixing broken code; it was about rebuilding trust. Technology had changed; now the leadership approach needed to, too. This moment was a turning point. WynnTech's team realized that their ambitious digital initiative wasn't failing because of technical flaws—it was faltering because human needs had been sidelined.

WynnTech's new platform rollout wasn't a technology story; it was a trust story. The teams who designed with end users from the start experienced far fewer setbacks. The difference was empathy built into process.

In the earlier chapters, we explored reflection, alignment, and modeling as leadership practices. Digital transformation tests all of them at once. It exposes how systems treat people, as participants or as data points.

Why People Come First

Technology is a mirror of culture. If the culture is transactional, tools amplify transaction; if it's collaborative, tools amplify connection. The leader's task is to ensure the human pattern drives the digital one.

This chapter begins with that insight: Digital transformation is, at its heart, human transformation.

Core Concepts and Framing

When organizations underestimate human needs during technology roll-outs, resistance grows, adoption falters, and opportunities are lost. People don't resist technology; they resist being left behind.

Digital transformation initiatives often fail not because the technology doesn't work but because leaders underestimate the human journey beneath the change. In fast-paced, high-stakes rollouts, organizations like WynnTech tend to focus on timelines, features, and adoption metrics, assuming that if the platform is functional, engagement will follow. But what WynnTech discovered, and what many leaders face, is that digital transformation succeeds or falters based on trust, inclusion, and participation.

At its core, digital transformation is not just about deploying a new platform or automating workflows; it's about shifting mindsets, relationships, and emotional landscapes. When leaders fail to involve employees early, fears multiply: fear of being left behind, fear of losing relevance, fear of the unknown. Conversely, when leaders intentionally design change with people, not just for them, engagement deepens and adoption accelerates.

WynnTech's early missteps underscored three critical lessons:

- **Listen before you launch:** The team had prioritized speed over dialogue, missing early opportunities to surface concerns and aspirations.
- **Integrate empathy into design:** Mapping emotional and relational impacts revealed how the platform reshaped people's roles, routines, and sense of contribution.
- **Frame digital change as culture change:** Elena's leadership pivoted when she recognized that introducing new technology meant reshaping how people work, connect, and trust one another.

By centering people, leaders transform digital initiatives from being systems-driven projects into shared human journeys. When the "why" of the transformation connects to personal meaning, leaders no longer have to push adoption—they invite it.

Leadership Integration Spotlight

Digital transformation challenges leaders to model empathy, adaptability, and co-creation. At WynnTech, Nia, Marcus, and Elena each embodied different but complementary approaches to centering people (a great example in Table 9.1) during a high-stakes platform rollout:

Key Insight: When leaders align technology with human meaning, they transform digital initiatives from top-down directives into shared ownership experiences.

Reflection is only powerful when it informs what we do next. By connecting inner awareness with outer action, leaders can move from intention to meaningful change. The following exercise invites you to put these insights into practice, testing how your choices, language, and presence shape the human experience of digital transformation.

Practice-in-Action Exercise

Choose a recent or ongoing digital initiative in your organization. Invite your team to reflect on these three guiding questions together:

1. **What did we assume?**

   Identify expectations you had about how people would adopt or respond to the change.

Table 9.1 People-centered leadership

Leadership role	People-centered digital leadership in action
Project Leader Nia	Embedded empathy mapping into project timelines, ensuring every feature launch considered user experience and employee impact. She introduced "voice-of-the-user" forums where feedback loops were built into sprint reviews.
Change Leader Marcus	Used storytelling and personas to make the emotional journey visible, bridging the gap between system design and lived experience. By sharing user stories, he reframed adoption challenges as opportunities for connection.
Executive Leader Elena	Shifted the narrative by framing digital change as culture change. She hosted open forums where employees could express concerns and co-design rollout strategies, signaling adaptability at the highest level.

2. **Who did we miss?**
   Surface whose voices or perspectives weren't included in design or rollout decisions.

3. **What would we do differently?**
   Generate ideas for how to better integrate people's emotional, relational, and practical needs in future initiatives.

Document your insights as a group and identify one immediate action you can take to improve alignment between technology and human experience.

Host This Conversation

While individual reflection is valuable, meaningful transformation happens when we make sense together. Hosting an open conversation with your team, or across functions, invites stories and perspectives that data alone can't capture.

- **Who benefits most, and least, from this digital change?**
- **Where might efficiency goals unintentionally erode connection or trust?**
- **How will we measure success in human terms?**

Chapter Closing Reflection

Digital transformation is more than deploying new technologies—it's about inviting people into a shared future. When leaders focus on human experience, trust grows, adoption accelerates, and systems evolve with the people they serve.

In the next chapter, we step into the bigger picture: how leaders sustain transformation by cultivating adaptive, learning-oriented organizations. Chapter 10 explores what it means to lead at scale, where the focus shifts from managing individual projects or systems to building a culture of continuous sensemaking, resilience, and innovation.

CHAPTER 10

The Inner Work of Systemic Change

Systems don't change because of frameworks; they change because people within them become more self-aware, connected, and courageous. This final chapter integrates presence, practice, and projects into one living system of people-centered transformation.

Learning Outcomes

By the end of this chapter, you will be able to:

- Synthesize the Leadership Integration Model and Dual-Lens Framework as a cohesive system.
- Reflect on how personal transformation enables organizational change.
- Identify next steps to sustain learning and dialogue beyond this book.

Leadership Lens: Starting from Within

Elena closed her laptop and stared at her reflection in the dark monitor. For the first time, she realized transformation wasn't about changing others—it was about changing herself.

Elena sat alone in the quiet of the WynnTech atrium long after the leadership session ended. The glass walls reflected the city's evening lights, but her thoughts were turned inward.

The team had spent the afternoon reviewing digital adoption metrics, upticks, drop-offs, usage patterns. But what stayed with her

---

weren't the data; it was a story Marcus shared. One of the frontline technicians had confided that he no longer recognized his role. "The system changed, but no one asked me how I work."

Elena realized, with sharp clarity, that systemic change wasn't just about rolling out solutions; it was about transforming the conditions that shape how people experience work. That required a different kind of leadership, one grounded not in control, but in presence, reflection, and letting go.

She opened her notebook and wrote just three words: *Start within first.*

Systemic change begins not with structures or strategies but with leaders themselves. "Starting within first" means reflecting on personal values, assumptions, and emotional patterns before attempting to influence the larger system. Leaders who align their inner narrative with their outer actions create the credibility and presence needed to inspire trust. By cultivating self-awareness and emotional agility, they become better equipped to engage complex dynamics, hold space for multiple perspectives, and guide transformation in ways that are authentic and sustainable.

Months later, WynnTech looked different. Meetings were quieter, but conversations went deeper. Metrics still mattered, yet so did meaning. Elena paused at the window overlooking the production floor and smiled—the work was still complex, but now, it felt human.

Core Concepts and Framing

Presence. Practice. Projects. These three anchors have guided our journey. Presence roots leadership in awareness; practice turns awareness into habit; projects translate habit into systemic results. When these align, transformation becomes self-sustaining because it lives in people, not in plans.

Systemic change is often viewed through structures, processes, and strategies, yet its deepest leverage point begins within the leader. When organizations face complexity, the instinct is to act outwardly, reorganizing teams, implementing new technologies, or redesigning systems. But these changes rarely take hold without parallel inner work: surfacing mental models, clarifying personal values, and cultivating the capacity to hold ambiguity.

Starting within doesn't mean withdrawing from the external system; it means developing narrative awareness, the ability to recognize the stories we tell ourselves about success, failure, power, and possibility. These stories shape decisions, relationships, and, ultimately, culture. Leaders who slow down to examine their assumptions unlock new options for action that go beyond default patterns.

This chapter explores three interconnected practices:

1. **Inner Alignment**
   Connecting personal values and purpose with organizational intent creates a foundation for authentic leadership.
2. **Narrative Awareness**
   Recognizing the unspoken stories shaping our choices allows leaders to challenge limiting beliefs and foster collective meaning-making.
3. **Systemic Leadership**
   Leaders act as sensemakers within complex systems, embodying the change they seek and creating conditions where others can thrive.

Transformation that lasts begins with the courage to look inward, and from there, to engage the system as a whole with greater clarity, empathy, and intentionality.

Before systemic change can take root, leaders must first turn inward. This chapter highlights how inner work, cultivating self-awareness, reframing personal narratives, and aligning values with actions, sets the foundation for sustainable transformation. At WynnTech, the journey of leading change became inseparable from the personal growth of its leaders. The following spotlight illustrates how Nia, Marcus, and Elena modeled this process in distinct yet interconnected ways.

Leadership Integration Spotlight

Project Leader—Nia: Cultivating Self-Awareness in Uncertainty

Nia journals daily to capture moments of tension and clarity in her leadership role. When she notices patterns, like avoiding conflict during team meetings, she uses reflective prompts to explore what drives that discomfort. Through this practice, she begins leading with greater transparency and courage, modeling openness for her team.

Change Leader—Marcus: Reframing Personal Narratives

Marcus leads cross-functional sessions but struggles with the emotional weight of the transformation. In coaching sessions, he explores the story he tells himself about always needing to "have the answers." Letting go of this belief allows him to step into a facilitator role, empowering others to contribute insights and solutions.

Executive Leader—Elena: Aligning Personal and Organizational Purpose

Elena reflects on whether her decisions signal the values she wants WynnTech to embody. By sharing her own moments of misalignment openly with the leadership team, she fosters psychological safety and demonstrates that leadership is a learning journey. Her modeling encourages others to examine how personal values and organizational goals intersect.

Let's take a look at all three leaders (Table 10.1) and their inner work efforts for encouraging personal exploration.

Table 10.1 Inner work driving systemic change

Leader	Inner work focus	Practical actions	Ripple effect on systemic change
Nia *(Project Leader)*	Cultivating self-awareness in uncertainty	Journals daily to recognize patterns of avoidance and courage; shares insights with her team	Builds transparency, encourages open dialogue, and fosters trust in project teams
Marcus *(Change Leader)*	Reframing personal narratives	Challenges his belief that he must "always have the answers" through coaching and team facilitation	Creates space for collective problem-solving and empowers diverse voices
Elena *(Executive Leader)*	Aligning personal and organizational purpose	Reflects on her decision-making and openly acknowledges moments of misalignment during leadership forums	Models vulnerability, strengthens psychological safety, and signals culture change

Practice-in-Action Exercise

Let me suggest you integrate your inner work into your leadership practice. Over the next week, identify one personal belief or habit that limits how you lead systemic change. Journal about the assumptions behind it, experiment with one small shift, and notice how others respond.

This ties back to our theme of presence and connects personal transformation to systemic impact.

Host This Conversation

Use a final dialogic prompt to encourage collective reflection:

- **"Where are we asking our teams to change without doing our own inner work first?"**
- **"What would it look like to make reflection as much a leadership practice as strategy?"**

Change doesn't begin with the system. It begins with the stories we tell, the conversations we host, and the presence we bring into every interaction. Through the dual lenses of inner experience and external dialogue, we've explored how leaders like Nia, Marcus, and Elena navigated the complexities of transformation, sometimes faltering, always learning.

Sustainable change emerges not from control but from co-creation. It lives in the space between practice and possibility, between what we know and what we're willing to learn. Whether you are leading a project, shaping culture, or setting strategic direction, your presence is the starting point.

The call to action is simple but profound: start within, act with others, and keep listening. Systems change because people do—one conversation, one choice, one commitment at a time.

Epilogue: A Year Later at WynnTech

The glass-walled atrium buzzed softly with the hum of conversation as employees trickled into the newly redesigned collaboration space. A year ago, this same room had been heavy with silence and suspicion. Today, laughter threaded through the air.

Nia stood by the coffee station, glancing at a whiteboard where someone had scrawled *"Stories Matter"* in bright blue marker, a phrase that had become their unofficial mantra. Marcus joined her, holding two mugs of coffee, his easy grin returning after months of hard-won trust-building.

"Remember where we were last year?" he asked.

Nia nodded. "No one would even speak up in these sessions. Now we can't get them to stop sharing."

Across the room, Elena was deep in conversation with a junior developer, her blazer slung over the back of a chair, her posture relaxed and open. She listened more than she spoke now, something she had once admitted didn't come naturally.

The company hadn't avoided every setback. Deadlines were still missed, disagreements still surfaced, and uncertainty still lingered. But something had shifted. WynnTech was no longer a collection of disconnected projects and anxious silos. It had become a learning organization, one where people trusted their voices would be heard and where change was something they did with each other, not to each other.

As Marcus glanced around the room, he caught Nia's eye and smiled. "We're not done," he said quietly.

Nia returned the smile. "No. But we know how to do the work now. Together."

Closing Reflection: Your Next Conversation

Transformation doesn't happen all at once. It begins in the quiet moments where you choose to pause, listen, and make meaning together. You've explored stories of trust, resistance, dialogue, and alignment, but the real work begins with your next conversation.

As a leader, you are always signaling what matters, not just through plans and strategies, but through the presence you bring and the stories you invite. Every choice—to ask a deeper question, to make space for another voice, to model vulnerability—becomes part of the system you are shaping.

There is no single roadmap for change. But there are practices you can return to again and again: listening with intention, leading with empathy, and aligning your actions with your values. These are the anchors that will sustain you and your teams through complexity and uncertainty.

As you complete this book, the next conversation begins. Each system you influence—team, community, organization—is a place to practice people-centered transformation. The more we lead through presence, practice, and projects, the more our systems become capable of humanity at scale. The next chapter isn't in this book. It's in the story you create, with your people, your projects, and your purpose.

Appendixes

Appendixes

APPENDIX A

Leadership Integration Model in Practice

The **Leadership Integration Model** is strongly supported by emerging research and practice across organizational transformation, leadership development, and systems thinking. This model invites leaders to ask deeper questions: How are we showing up together? Where are we aligned or disconnected? What tensions are surfacing, and what do they reveal about our system?

Why the Leadership Integration Model Matters

In today's complex business environment, traditional leadership models, centered on hierarchy, individual heroism, or technical expertise, are increasingly inadequate (McKinsey 2025). The Leadership Integration Model offers a timely and necessary shift: It emphasizes distributed leadership, cultural alignment, and reflective practice across project, change, and executive roles. This model is not just a framework; it's a strategy for activating leadership as a systemic capability.

- Research from the World Economic Forum and Leadership Circle shows that integrated leadership, balancing relational and autonomous capacities, correlates with better business outcomes, greater adaptability, and healthier organizational cultures (Forbes 2024).
- Leaders who harmonize inner development (self-awareness, mindset, and presence) with outer leadership (dialogue, coordination, and storytelling) are better equipped to navigate complexity and foster transformation.

Distinctive Features of the Model

- **Role-Based Integration**: Unlike models that centralize leadership in the executive tier, this framework distributes leadership across project, change, and executive domains. It aligns with findings from *Forbes* and *Harvard Business Review* that successful transformations require coordinated contributions from multiple leadership sources (Forbes 2024; Harvard Business Review 2025).
- **Inner–Outer Leadership Bridge**: The model's integration of inner development with outer practice reflects the "inside-out" leadership journey advocated by McKinsey. Leaders must evolve personally to lead systemically (McKinsey 2025).
- **Relational and Reflective Practice**: The model's emphasis on reflection, sensemaking, and relational awareness is echoed in research on emotional journeys in transformation. Leaders who engage in reflective practice and build psychological safety are more likely to succeed in change initiatives (Harvard Business Review 2025).
- **Cultural Modeling and Alignment**: The model's focus on cultural dynamics is supported by the Innovative Leadership Transformation Model, which stresses the need to align leadership, culture, and systems for sustainable change (LeadsLikeA 2025).

Implications for Business Leaders

- **Executive leaders** must model vulnerability, presence, and alignment, not just strategy.
- **Change leaders** must facilitate sensemaking and emotional resilience across teams.
- **Project leaders** must coordinate delivery with cultural awareness and relational intelligence.

This Appendix gives readers a reference summarizing the key practices, tools, and leadership roles introduced throughout the book. It integrates:

- Lens 1—The inner experience of leading change
- Lens 2—The outer conversations shaping systems
- Project, Change, and Executive Leadership perspectives
- Core tools and reflection prompts

Leadership Integration Framework

Leadership dimension	Lens 1: Inner experience	Lens 2: Conversations and actions	Key tools	Leader spotlight
Clarity and Alignment	Explore personal values, purpose, and meaning	Facilitate conversations that align vision, goals, and actions	Alignment Arc Model	Project: Nia Change: Marcus Executive: Elena
Trust and Resistance	Recognize fears and assumptions beneath resistance	Create safe spaces for dialogue and shared problem-solving	Trust Diagnostic + Conversation Audit	Same as above
Story and Dialogue	Notice personal narratives that shape decisions	Use storytelling to connect meaning, build empathy, and foster collaboration	Reflective Dialogue Guide	Same as above
Modeling Change	Examine gaps between beliefs and behaviors	Signal desired culture through consistent actions	Empathy Action Bridge	Same as above
Learning at the Edge	Embrace discomfort and self-doubt as pathways to growth	Normalize vulnerability within team dialogue and leadership practices	Growth Zone Reflection Matrix	Same as above
People in Digital Change	Reflect on assumptions about tech and human capacity	Prioritize emotional, relational, and behavioral impacts	Reflective Compass Map	Same as above

APPENDIX B

Dual-Lens Framework Overview

Integrating Leadership Experience and Conversational Function in People-Centered Transformation

This Appendix expands on the Dual-Lens Framework introduced in Chapter 1. It's designed as a quick-reference map for facilitators, teams, and leaders who want to connect internal awareness (Lens 1) with external action (Lens 2) in their daily work. It helps leaders understand how their internal awareness connects with their outward conversations. It links reflection with action, making leadership more intentional and connected.

Lens 1: Categories of Experience

In this book, you'll see these inner orientations appear in the WynnTech story.

Experience categories of conversation

Lens 1 category	Description
Strategically Intentional	Focused on clarifying direction, aligning teams, and communicating goals
Catalyst for Change	Motivated to disrupt the status quo and inspire growth or transformation
Mindful Awareness	Attuned to emotional dynamics, complexity, and reflective insight
Building Shared Commitment	Centered on trust, inclusion, and fostering relational connection
Guiding the Change	Holding the broader system view and integrating meaning with coordinated action

Lens 2: Functional Purposes of Conversation

These conversational functions surface when Nia, Marcus, and Elena translate insight into dialogue.

Functional categories of conversation

Lens 2 function	Description	Lens 1 alignment
As Transmission	Delivering information and clarifying expectations. Often directive.	Strategically Intentional
As Transformation	Reframing mindsets, catalyzing commitment, and shifting belief systems	Catalyst for Change
As Sensemaking	Facilitating reflection, surfacing ambiguity, and co-creating meaning	Mindful Awareness
As Relationship	Building trust, safety, and belonging through emotional presence and empathy	Building Shared Commitment
As Alignment/Transformation	Integrating perspectives and sustaining system-wide momentum. A synthesis of insight and execution.	Guiding the Change

How the Lenses Work Together

When combined with the Leadership Integration Model, the Dual-Lens Framework shows how aligned roles are brought to life through reflective presence. This integrated framework reveals how leadership identity and impact are interwoven. Leaders don't just communicate—they shape outcomes by how they show up, what they notice, and how they listen, speak, and act. The table below illustrates this:

Dual-Lens Framework overview

Lens 1 experience	Lens 2 function	Integrated purpose
Strategically Intentional	As Transmission	Clarify priorities, reinforce alignment, and ensure visibility
Catalyst for Change	As Transformation	Disrupt inertia, inspire momentum, and expand possibility

Lens 1 experience	Lens 2 function	Integrated purpose
Mindful Awareness	As Sensemaking	Hold space for reflection, enable insight, and navigate complexity
Building Shared Commitment	As Relationship	Build relational trust, foster engagement, and co-own the journey
Guiding the Change	As Alignment/ Transformation	Integrate purpose, roles, and systems for sustained organizational transformation

Applications in Leadership Practice

Throughout **How People Change Organizations**, this framework appears whenever reflection turns into coordinated action, whether in team dialogue, coaching, or systemic alignment. This framework is used throughout the book to analyze leadership conversations at the project, change, and executive levels. It enables:

- Team dialogue facilitation grounded in shared purpose and role clarity
- Leadership coaching focused on deepening reflexivity and impact
- Project reviews and retrospectives informed by relational and narrative cues
- Organizational transformation efforts that align internal leader development with external strategic direction

Closing Note

The Dual-Lens Framework is not a script; it's a reflective map. Leaders will move across these categories depending on the moment, context, and complexity of the challenge. What matters is not staying in one mode, but knowing where you are, and why, so you can better lead others through change with clarity, care, and coherence. Its purpose in this book is to help leaders notice themselves in the conversations that shape organizational change.

APPENDIX C

The Reflection Compass

The Reflection Compass is designed to help people-centered leaders build reflective capacity by intentionally scanning four key domains of experience: Self, Others, System, and Purpose. In the midst of complex change, leaders often default to familiar responses without noticing the assumptions, pressures, or blind spots driving their actions. This tool slows the moment down, allowing for grounded insight and renewed intentionality.

How to Use the Reflection Compass

Use this compass during or after significant decisions, emotionally charged meetings, or project turning points. Ask yourself the guiding questions in each quadrant to explore your leadership stance and uncover new insight. You can write responses in a journal, share them in peer reflection, or use them to guide a coaching conversation.

Reflection Quadrants

SELF: What's happening within me?
- What emotions or stories are present for me right now?
- Where am I feeling reactive, guarded, or open?
- What past experiences might be influencing my current response?

OTHERS: What am I noticing about others?
- Who seems activated, quiet, resistant, or engaged?
- What assumptions am I making about their behavior?
- How am I influencing or being influenced by the group dynamic?

SYSTEM: What's happening around us?
- What broader pressures, policies, or patterns are at play?
- What's reinforcing the current situation?

- What power or cultural dynamics might be shaping this interaction?

PURPOSE: What do we care about most?
  - What is the deeper purpose of this moment?
  - What future am I helping to shape right now?
  - How do I want to show up, regardless of outcome?

Example in Practice

After a tense stakeholder meeting about delayed timelines, Nia takes 10 minutes to pause and use the Reflection Compass Tool described on page 35.

SELF: I felt frustrated and rushed. I was trying to stay composed but noticed my jaw was tight and I kept interrupting.

OTHERS: Marcus looked concerned, and Elena kept glancing at the clock. I assumed they were disappointed, but maybe they were just trying to manage their own tensions.

SYSTEM: We're under pressure from the board, and our hybrid model is still uneven. That's creating unclear roles and unspoken stress.

PURPOSE: Our goal is not just on-time delivery but a healthy team and a values-aligned rollout. I want to be someone who models calm even when the stakes are high.

Why It Matters

Taking time to use the Reflection Compass may seem like a pause in momentum, but it's actually a catalyst for more intentional leadership. By surfacing internal reactions, relational cues, systemic dynamics, and shared purpose, leaders gain clarity not only about what's happening but also about how they want to lead through it. The outcome isn't just insight but also its impact. This tool builds the self-awareness and grounded presence needed to lead complex transformation with empathy, courage, and authenticity.

APPENDIX D

The WynnTech Case Study

A Unified Approach to Change Leadership

This narrative case study is featured across all four books in the *Conversations That Inspire Change* series:

- Empowering Strategic Change: Conversation-Focused Project Leadership
- People-Centered Transformation: Transforming Systems Through Presence, Practice, and People
- Leading Change from Within—coming soon
- The Inner Work of Transformation—coming soon

The WynnTech case highlights a core truth: Transformation is not just about technology—it is about people, relationships, and the conversations that make change possible. This story follows the experience of three interconnected leaders—a project manager, a change leader, and an executive—who navigate a high-stakes transformation effort with empathy, reflection, and purpose.

The Context

WynnTech, a mid-sized technology firm with a respected legacy, embarked on a digital transformation aimed at overhauling outdated systems, improving responsiveness, and fostering a more agile and inclusive culture. Early in the initiative, however, it became clear that this was not merely a technical upgrade; it was a human journey. Success would depend on aligning hearts and minds as much as platforms and processes.

Progress Update: WynnTech's Transformation So Far

Since the early days of their digital transformation, WynnTech has moved beyond system upgrades and process efficiencies to embrace a deeper, more people-centered approach to change. The leadership trio— Nia, Marcus, and Elena—each took vital steps to reframe their roles: from directing outcomes to facilitating meaning, trust, and inclusion. Through adaptive governance, emotionally resonant storytelling, and a shift toward vulnerability in executive leadership, they transformed their initial resistance into momentum. Project teams began to ask better questions, engage more authentically, and surface systemic challenges that had previously gone unspoken. What began as a "transformation initiative" evolved into a cultural shift built on shared values and reflective practice.

Today, WynnTech's transformation is no longer a project with a deadline; it's a practice embedded in how they lead, decide, and grow together. Employee engagement is up, cross-functional collaboration is more natural, and feedback is welcomed as a driver of evolution rather than a sign of failure. Nia continues to refine inclusive delivery frameworks, Marcus has trained internal storytelling facilitators to carry the work forward, and Elena's leadership presence now models learning, rather than command. With a more aligned and empathetic leadership culture in place, Wynn-Tech is now positioned to take the next step: not just sustaining transformation but also living it, through every conversation, relationship, and decision that shapes their future.

Three Roles in Reflective Leadership

Nia Thompson—Project Leadership

Nia, the project manager, brought an inclusive lens to delivery. She introduced adaptive governance models, created cross-functional planning teams, and embedded feedback loops that prioritized equity and psychological safety. When middle managers expressed concern about a perceived top-down approach, Nia adjusted timelines and opened up new channels for dialogue. By slowing down to listen, she enabled others to step into ownership and aligned project delivery with people-first values.

Marcus Lee—Change Leadership

Marcus, the change leader, served as the strategic storyteller of the transformation. He facilitated dialogue sessions that helped teams articulate fears, revisit past failures, and co-create a forward-looking narrative. Drawing on tools from Empowering Strategic Change: Conversation-Focused Project Leadership, Marcus reframed the effort from "systems implementation" to "purposeful evolution." His use of metaphor and emotion made space for deeper engagement and helped teams connect with the meaning behind the change.

Elena Patel—Executive Leadership

As WynnTech's COO, Elena initially focused on adoption metrics, efficiencies, and timelines. Through executive coaching and guided reflection, she began to shift her focus inward. Inspired by practices from Empowering Strategic Change: Conversation-Focused Project Leadership, she embraced vulnerability, hosted monthly learning sessions, and reframed her role from directive leader to learning partner. Her personal growth journey helped model a new kind of leadership, one grounded in emotional intelligence, humility, and presence.

Bringing It All Together

Together, Nia, Marcus, and Elena created a powerful model of integrated leadership. Their alignment, grounded in shared purpose and reflective practice, helped the transformation take root in meaningful and sustainable ways.

- Strategy was communicated through values-based narrative.
- Systems became more inclusive, flexible, and responsive.
- Psychological safety moved from aspiration to daily practice.
- Inner development was embraced as a driver of organizational change.

Outcomes

- Twenty-two percent increase in employee engagement
- Faster adoption of digital tools with fewer rework cycles
- Reduced resistance and increased trust in leadership
- Emergence of cross-functional change champions

WynnTech's story will serve as a guiding case across all four books in the series, demonstrating how project, change, and executive leaders can integrate outer strategy with inner clarity, and conversation with action.

Case Study Reflection Guide—Leadership Roles in Action

1. **Project Leadership (Nia Thompson)**
   - How did Nia use inclusive practices to manage resistance?
   - What governance structures supported psychological safety?
   - As a project leader, how do you balance structure with adaptability?

     Reflection Prompt:

     When I'm under pressure to deliver, I tend to…

     What mindset helps me remain people-centered even when outcomes are at stake?

2. **Change Leadership (Marcus Lee)**
   - How did Marcus use story and dialogue to shift mindsets?
   - What helped him surface the emotional undercurrents of change?
   - How do you co-create the narrative of change with your team?

     Reflection Prompt:

     Whose voices or stories are missing in my current change work?

     What narrative do I need to release to move forward with clarity?

3. **Executive Leadership (Elena Patel)**
   - What was significant about Elena's inner shift?
   - How did her transformation influence others?

- ○ How do senior leaders demonstrate emotional intelligence in practice?

  Reflection Prompt:

  What kind of presence do I bring to the room as a leader?

  When I become reactive, how do I recover and realign with my values?

Reflective Dialogue Guide

A Framework for Storytelling, Listening, and Collective Sensemaking

Framework for storytelling, listening, and collective sensemaking

Step	Purpose	Leadership practice	Guiding questions
1. Open with Story and Set the Stage	Create psychological safety and shared intent.	Frame the purpose of the dialogue, clarify what's at stake, and model openness.	"Why are we here?" "What are we trying to make sense of together?"
2. Invite Storytelling, Listen to Understand	Surface experiences and emotions to locate meaning.	Use open-ended prompts that invite diverse voices and perspectives.	"What's one moment from this change journey that has stayed with you?" "What's a word that captures how you're feeling right now?"
3. Notice the Themes	Surface patterns, hopes, and concerns emerging across stories.	Links individual meaning to collective insight.	"What I'm hearing is … Did I get that right?"
4. Connect to Purpose	Identify shared meaning across different experiences.	Synthesize themes and highlight points of resonance or divergence.	"What themes are emerging in our stories?" "Where are we aligned, and where do we need to explore further?"
5. Translate to Action	Move from shared meaning to aligned next steps.	Co-create commitments and connect them to the broader purpose.	"What do we need to do differently based on what we've heard?" "What will we take forward together?"

How to Use This Guide

- **Project Leaders** can integrate it into sprint reviews or team stand-ups to uncover blockers and opportunities.
- **Change Leaders** can host reflective sessions to process emotions and build alignment.
- **Executives** can join sessions as listeners to foster trust and model curiosity.

Glossary

Change Fatigue
A state of emotional and cognitive exhaustion caused by repeated or poorly managed organizational change, often leading to resistance, burnout, or disengagement.

Dialogic Mindset
An orientation to change leadership that emphasizes listening, emergence, and participation, as opposed to directive or command-control approaches.

Dual-Lens Framework
A leadership model that integrates two essential perspectives: Lens 1 (internal experiences such as meaning-making, identity, and emotion) and Lens 2 (external conversations, actions, and systemic dynamics). It is used throughout the book to bridge personal self-awareness with organizational impact.

Empathy Action Bridge
A tool for linking awareness and action, translating empathy into visible leadership behaviors that reinforce shared purpose.

Growth Zone Reflection Matrix
A self-awareness tool that helps leaders identify when they are in their comfort zone, stretch zone, or stress zone—supporting intentional risk-taking and personal development.

Leadership Integration Spotlight
Recurring features that show how different leadership roles (Project, Change, and Executive) collaborate to support systemic transformation.

Learning at the Edge
The practice of leaning into discomfort and uncertainty as a signal of growth, both individually and organizationally.

Lens 1 (Internal Experience)
Refers to the inner world of the leader, their values, emotions, sense of purpose, and personal alignment as they navigate change and make meaning of events.

Lens 2 (External Conversation)
Focuses on observable behaviors, interactions, conversations, and system-level patterns that shape organizational culture, decision-making, and outcomes.

People-Centered Transformation
An approach to organizational or digital change that places people, their experiences, relationships, and capacity to contribute, at the center of all transformation efforts.

Practice-in-Action Exercises
Short, structured activities integrated into the book that invite readers to apply concepts directly in their leadership or team contexts.

Psychological Safety
A team or organizational climate where individuals feel safe to express themselves, raise concerns, ask questions, and admit mistakes without fear of negative consequences.

Narrative Leadership
An approach to leadership that uses story as a tool to foster empathy, build shared understanding, and align individuals and teams around a common vision for change.

Reflective Dialogue
A facilitated group practice that invites storytelling, deep listening, and inquiry to surface hidden perspectives, generate insight, and co-create meaning across teams or stakeholder groups.

Resistance as a Message
A reframe of resistance from a barrier to be overcome into a signal that reveals unmet needs, broken trust, or systemic misalignment that needs to be addressed.

Story-Based Sensemaking
The use of narrative to interpret complexity, connect disparate experiences, and guide collective learning and decision-making.

Systems Thinking
A lens for understanding organizations as interconnected systems, emphasizing the importance of patterns, relationships, and root causes over isolated problems.

References

Argyris, Chris, and Donald A. Schön. 1978. *Organizational Learning: A Theory of Action Perspective.* Addison-Wesley.

Bass, Bernard M., and Ronald E. Riggio. 2006. *Transformational Leadership.* 2nd ed. Lawrence Erlbaum Associates.

Bonterre, Michelle. 2025. "Why Psychological Safety Is the Hidden Engine Behind Innovation and Transformation." *Harvard Business Impact Insights*, July 29. l.l https://www.harvardbusiness.org/insight/why-psychological-safety-is-the-hidden-engine-behind-innovation-and-transformation/.

Brown, Brené. 2018. *Dare to Lead: Brave Work. Tough Conversations. Whole Hearts.* Random House.

Bushe, Gervase R., and Robert J. Marshak. 2016. "The Dialogic Mindset: Leading Emergent Change in a Complex World." *Organization Development Journal* 34 (1): 37–65.

Denning, Stephen. 2005. *The Leader's Guide to Storytelling: Mastering the Art and Discipline of Business Narrative.* Jossey-Bass.

Dickerson, Craig. 2025. "From Emotional Triggers to Values-Based Leadership: A Practical Framework." *Harvard Business Review*, July 1. Accessed August 29, 2025. https://www.harvardbusiness.org/insight/from-emotional-triggers-to-values-based-leadership-a-practical-framework/.

Edmondson, Amy C. 2019. *The Fearless Organization: Creating Psychological Safety in the Workplace for Learning, Innovation, and Growth.* Wiley.

Edmondson, Amy C., and Michaela J. Kerrissey. 2025. "What People Get Wrong about Psychological Safety." *Harvard Business Review*, May–June. https://hbr.org/2025/05/what-people-get-wrong-about-psychological-safety.

Forbes. 2024. "6 Powerful People Practices for Leading Through Change." Accessed August 28, 2025. https://www.forbes.com/sites/brentgleeson/2024/11/07/6-powerful-people-practices-for-leading-through-change/.

Harvard Business Review. 2025. "The Power of Mattering at Work." Accessed August 28, 2025. https://hbr.org/2025/05/the-power-of-mattering-at-work.

Harvard Business Review. 2025. "Why You Need Systems Thinking Now." Accessed August 28, 2025. https://hbr.org/2025/09/why-you-need-systems-thinking-now.

Kraemer, Harry M. 2025. "Do We Really Need Values to Lead?" *Forbes*, March 11. Accessed August 29, 2025. https://www.forbes.com/sites/harrykraemer/2025/03/11/do-we-really-need-values-to-lead/.

Leads Like A. 2025. "Leading Off: How Will Technology Transform People Management?" Accessed August 28, 2025. https://www.mckinsey.com/~/media/mckinsey/email/leadingoff/2025/05/01/2025-05-05b.html.

Maitlis, Sally, and Marlys K. Christianson. 2014. "Sensemaking in Organizations: Taking Stock and Moving Forward." *Academy of Management Annals* 8 (1): 57–125.

McKinsey & Company. 2025. "A New Operating Model for People Management: More Personal, More Tech, More Human." Accessed August 28, 2025. https://www.mckinsey.com/capabilities/people-and-organizational-performance/our-insights/a-new-operating-model-for-people-management-more-personal-more-tech-more-human#/.

Petrie, Nick. 2014. *Future Trends in Leadership Development.* Center for Creative Leadership.

Randel, Amy E., Michelle A. Dean, Jessica G. Ehrhart, and Aparna Joshi. 2018. "Inclusive Leadership: Realizing Positive Outcomes Through Belongingness and Being Valued for Uniqueness." *Human Resource Management Review* 28 (2): 190–203.

Santos, Catarina M., Sjir Uitdewilligen, Lex van der Vegt, and Ana Margarida Passos. 2025. "Directed but Reflecting: Guided Team Reflexivity as an Intervention to Foster Team Performance Improvement Under Directive Leadership." *Group & Organization Management,* https://doi.org/10.1177/10596011251323984.

Senge, Peter M. 1995. "Leading Learning Organizations." In *The Leader of the Future,* edited by Frances Hesselbein, Marshall Goldsmith, and Richard Beckhard, 41–58. Jossey-Bass. Originally published as *Leading Learning Organizations.* MIT Center for Organizational Learning Research Monograph.

Senge, Peter, Hal Hamilton, and John Kania. 2015. "The Dawn of System Leadership." *Stanford Social Innovation Review* 13 (1): 27–33.

Snowden, David J., and Mary E. Boone. 2007. "A Leader's Framework for Decision Making." *Harvard Business Review,* November. https://hbr.org/2007/11/a-leaders-framework-for-decision-making?utm_medium=paidsearch&utm.

Weick, Karl E. 1995. *Sensemaking in Organizations.* Sage Publications.

Weick, Karl E., Kathleen M. Sutcliffe, and David Obstfeld. 2005. "Organizing and the Process of Sensemaking." *Organization Science* 16 (4): 409–421.

Back Cover Story

In an era where transformation is constant, many change efforts still fall short. Not because of poor strategy but because they overlook the one thing that makes change possible: human experience. *How People Change Organizations* reframes transformation as a deeply human process, one built not just on systems and plans but also on presence, practice, and people-centered leadership.

Grounded in decades of experience and informed by the Leadership Integration Model and the Dual-Lens Framework, this book brings together theory and action, insight and application. With real-life vignettes, reflective tools, and a full case study of WynnTech's digital transformation, it explores how leaders at every level, project, change, and executive, can:

- Cultivate presence and clarity in the face of complexity.
- Build trust and dialogue through practice-based leadership.
- Align strategy with lived experience to foster meaningful, sustainable change.
- Reframe resistance, foster psychological safety, and honor human impact.
- Lead systems change without losing sight of the people within them.

From frontline managers to senior executives, this book is a call to lead differently, by listening, engaging, and showing up fully. Whether you're guiding digital transformation, navigating cultural shifts, or building inclusive practices, you'll find practical guidance to activate reflection, reimagine leadership, and create lasting impact.

About the Author

 **Dr. Kathy Cowan Sahadath** is a business leader, educator, and author with more than 30 years of experience in strategic project and change management, organizational development, and leadership transformation. She has held senior roles across complex organizations, advising executive teams on navigating workforce disruption, digital transformation, and cultural alignment.

Kathy holds degrees in psychology, an MBA in project management, an MA in human and organizational development, and a PhD in human and organizational systems, where her research explored how leaders use conversation to shape change. She has also taught extensively in higher education, weaving together adult learning theory, reflective practice, and systems thinking.

An accomplished novelist and consultant, Kathy integrates storytelling with leadership expertise to design inclusive, people-centered learning experiences. Her work bridges research and practice, offering leaders fresh insight into the conversations that truly drive transformation.

Index

Adaptive learning, leadership, 87
Aligning culture, purpose, and
    performance, 43–52
Alignment Arc, 49–50, 77
Awareness, modeling change, 83

Brown, Brené, 87

Change fatigue, 25
Change leader, 67, 104
    micro-vignette 2, 56–57
Change leadership, 4–6, 10, 34, 35,
    121, 123, 124
Choreographing leadership, 9
Collective learning, 55
Collective sensemaking, 69, 71–72,
    127–128

Dialogic leadership, 61, 66
Dickerson, Craig, 79
Digital transformation, 95–99
Discomfort, growth requires, 86–87
Dual-Lens Framework, 1, 3, 29, 34,
    46–47, 58, 79, 80, 82, 86,
    115–117
    Alignment Arc, 50
    external conversation, 8
    integrating presence and impact, 11
    internal experience, 8
    for people-centered leadership, 7–9
    reflection prompts, 25–26, 51
    weave of transformation, 11–12
Dual-lens reflection, 82–83

Edmondson, Amy, 80, 87
Emotional intelligence, 14
Empathy, 21–22
    in action, 23–24
    Action Bridge, 24–25
    conversation, 27
    Dual-Lens Framework, 25–26
    Elena's listening tour, 25
    leadership lens, 21–22

reframe meeting, 26
    as strategic capacity, 22–23
Enterprise resource planning (ERP)
    system, 60
Executive leader, 67, 104
    micro-vignette 3, 57
Executive leadership, 4, 6, 10–11, 34,
    35, 123–125

Growth, 85–91
The Growth Zone Reflection Matrix,
    88, 89

Inner alignment, 103
Integrated leadership
    people-centered transformation, 12
    power of, 7, 123

Key Performance Indicators (KPIs), 13
Kraemer, Harry, 79

Lead transformation
    assumptions, 13
    leadership as integration, not
        isolation, 6–7
    Leadership Integration
        Model, 1, 3–6
    myths, 13–14
    paradigm shift, 12–14
    as technical exercise, 4
Leadership
    applications in, 117
    choreographing, 9
    conversation, 18–19
    dialogue, 66
    as integration, 6–7
    reflection in, 33
    role spotlight, 17
    vulnerability and growth in
        adaptive learning, 87
        conversation reflection, 89
        discomfort, 86–87
        growth signal, 87

practice-in-action exercise, 90
reflection, 87–88
spiral of uncertainty, 85–86
strength, 87
WynnTech, 88–89
Leadership discipline, 29–39
Leadership Integration Model, 1, 3–6,
    34, 46–47, 80, 111–113, 116
    Alignment Arc, 50
    choreographing leadership, 9
    integrating presence and impact, 11
    storytelling, listening, and, 66–67
    weave of transformation, 11–12
Leadership Signals Map, 81–82
Lee, Marcus, 123, 124

Modeling
    change you seek, 77–84
    definition of, 78–79
    Dual-Lens Framework, 80
    dual-lens reflection, 82–83
    Leadership Integration Model, 80
    Leadership Signals Map, 81–82
    modeling behavior, 79
    presence under pressure, 79
    psychological safety, 80
    social learning, 80
    values-based leadership, 79
    who gets a seat at the table, 77–78
Modeling behavior, 79
Modeling change, 79, 82

Narrative awareness, 103

Patel, Elena, 123–125
People-centered leadership, 98
    Dual-Lens Framework for, 7–9
People-centered transformation, 12,
    17, 18, 19, 23, 101, 107,
    115–116
Project leader, 66, 103–104
    micro-vignette 1, 55–56
Project leadership, 4–5, 9–10, 34,
    35, 122–124
Psychological safety, 55, 80

Reflection, 87–88, 98, 99
    leadership discipline, 29–39
    in action, 35–36

alignment, 36–37
compass, how to use, 31–33
compass tool, 30–31
connecting to the models, 34
Nia's insights, 34–35
the power of pause, 29–30
using the tools, 37–39
The Reflection Compass, 15–17,
    30–33, 35, 119–120
Reflective Dialogue Guide, 67–68,
    72, 127–128
Reflective leadership, 15, 122–123
    begins with you, 18
Reflexivity, 55
Reframing resistance/rebuilding trust
    micro-vignette 1—project leader,
        55–56
    micro-vignette 2—change leader,
        56–57
    micro-vignette 3—executive leader,
        57–58
    practice-in-action exercise, 60
    research insight, 54–55
    when the pace feels too fast, 53–54
    Trust Diagnostic and Conversation
        Audit, 58
    WynnTech, 58–60

Self-reflection/clear value alignment, 79
Sensemaking practices
    dialogue, 63–73, 127–128
    listening, 63–73, 127–128
    storytelling, 63–73, 127–128
"Slow down to speed up" approach, 55
Social learning, 80
Systemic change, 101–107
Systemic leadership, 103
Systems thinking, 66, 111

Technology, 96, 97
Thompson, Nia, 122–124
Tools, 37–39, 58, 66
Transformation. *See* Lead
    transformation
    Alignment Arc, 49
    Dual-Lens Framework, 7
    Leadership Integration Model, 4
    modeling, 77–84
    paradigm shift, 12–14

Reflection Compass, 15–17
    stories, 66
    weave of, 11–12
    WynnTech, 32, 45, 58, 60, 70, 122
Trust Diagnostic and Conversation
        Audit, 58–59

Values-based leadership, 22, 79
Vulnerability, 85–91

Weick, Karl, 65
WynnTech, 1, 3–4, 88–89, 97, 98,
        101–106

board update, 32
bridging silos through story at,
        68–70
case study, 121–125
dialogue session, 65, 69
making sense together, 70–71
purpose, culture, and
        performance, 47
reflection in, 58–60
reflective leadership, 54
storytelling session, 72
tipping point, 47–49
trust gap, 60

www.ingramcontent.com/pod-product-compliance
Lightning Source LLC
Chambersburg PA
CBHW051526170526
45165CB00002B/620